"Whether you're sixteen or sixty, you will be intrigued and uplifted while reading *Butterfly in Brazil*. Glenn Packiam communicates age-old biblical truths in a wonderfully relevant style. You will be inspired to see significance in the mundane, and opportunity in seemingly small things. Prepare for your life to be changed, now and for eternity."

JOHN AND LISA BEVERE
Founders of Messenger International

"For a world drunk with immediacy, Glenn Packiam has a sobering message: a life worth living takes time and care. It's just the right insight at just the right moment. Glenn's ideas are serious, but his voice is light and bright, and he delivers on the book's promise to paint a picture of a life that counts."

PATTON DODD
Editor for Beliefnet and author of My Faith So Far:
A Story of Conversion and Confusion

"Glenn Packiam lives what he writes. Woven into his personal story is a message all generations need to hear. A word of faithfulness and a daily walk that brings about the dreams that God has for each believer. I gladly endorse this inspiring book and my friend who penned it."

PAUL BALOCHE
Worship Leader and Dove Award–winning songwriter

"*Butterfly in Brazil* presents a heart-moving, level-headed approach to changing the world. Every young person who wants to create a lasting change should get their hands on this book."

DAVID PERKINS
Director of Desperation '07

"Glenn Packiam convincingly points us to what we dare not overlook: ordinary places and small steps. He does so because he knows that it is in those places and in that measure that those who follow Jesus can regularly bear witness that the Kingdom of God is at hand. The ministry of Jesus does not need spiritual stars nearly so much as it needs ordinary disciples demonstrating God's extraordinary grace in the plain places where we all live and where God's grace is so needed."

MARK LABBERTON
Pastor of First Presbyterian Church, Berkeley, California, and author of The Dangerous Act of Worship

Butterfly in Brazil

GLENN PACKIAM

Tyndale House Publishers, Inc.
Carol Stream, Illinois

Library of Congress Cataloging-in-Publication Data

Packiam, Glenn.
  Butterfly in Brazil : how your life can make a world of difference / Glenn Packiam.
    p. cm.
  Includes bibliographical references.
  ISBN-13: 978-1-4143-1329-0 (sc)
  ISBN-10: 1-4143-1329-2 (sc)
  1. Change—Religious aspects—Christianity. 2. Christian life. 3. Helping behavior—Religious aspects—Christianity. 4. Caring—Religious aspects—Christianity. I. Title.
  BV4509.5.P323 2007
  248.4—dc22   2007010800

To Holly, the companion of my soul and the love of my life:
You make even the ordinary seem out of this world.

To our dear daughters, Sophia and Norah.
May you change others' hearts the way you have changed mine.
Your world has just begun.

Contents

Acknowledgments

A book is a reflection of a life and the lessons learned along the way. In both the learning of these lessons and the writing of this book, I am immeasurably indebted to others. Here is a short list with just the beginnings of my immense gratitude.

To my matchless wife, Holly, for letting me burn the midnight oil, skip a few diaper changes, and read out loud to you. You have shown me what it means to be steady and to do small things well.

To Dad and Mom, for igniting my love for books, for helping me to see a big world and live a big life, and for showing me what full obedience to God looks like. I am proud to carry your name.

To Tracy, my sister, for stretching my brain around ideas much bigger than I am. Life is much better because I had your footsteps to follow.

To Bill and Roxanne, for taking me into your family and teaching me the way of the farm. Simplicity and steadiness are your gifts to me.

To Ross Parsley, for your leadership and friendship. You are a compass to me. Thank you for giving me the freedom and the faith to undertake this project, and for living out what we believe.

To Jon Egan, Jared Anderson, Aaron Stern, Brent Parsley, David Perkins, and Jeremiah Parks. You are my brothers, and these are the lessons we've learned together. I couldn't have asked for better company on the journey. Here's to the road ahead.

To Patton Dodd, for giving me the first glimmer of hope that these ideas might be something worth communicating, and for your encouragement along the way.

To Don Pape, for buying breakfast at the Cracker Barrel, and for being an early fan and a faithful friend.

To my new friends at Tyndale: Jon Farrar, for always being an advocate for me, and for being willing to take the chance. To Dave Lindstedt, Adam Graber, and Cara Lacey, for your relentless and ruthless work on the manuscript. You've made this a stronger book. To Travis, Keri, Kathy, and all the others, for working so hard and making this a great experience.

To the New Life Church family and all my friends and colleagues there: Through the mountains and the valleys, God remains faithful. I am so grateful for family like you.

1 beginnings

Beginnings are only as significant as their endings. A runner who doesn't win the race finds no consolation in a good start. Successful endings are often determined by the very ordinary moments in the middle.

Nevertheless, we're obsessed with beginnings—the start of a new project, a new relationship, a new book. Everybody wants to start a revolution; but nobody wants to fight to the last man standing.

1

We long to be extraordinary, to be remembered long after we're gone, to be part of something greater than ourselves, to leave a legacy; yet we don't want to go to work on Monday morning.

A life of humble beginnings can end with epic significance. One life can make a world of difference. There is a secret to how it occurs. It's not a secret because few people know it; it's a secret because few people *live* as if they know it.

This is a journey to the discovery of that secret.

But this is only the beginning.

2 storing up greatness

I had a strange childhood: I
grew up in a Christian home. That's
strange enough in itself, but what made
it interesting is the fact that I grew up
as a Christian in Malaysia, where there
are lots of different religions, ethnici-
ties, and blended cultures. Christians
account for ten to twelve percent of
the population, so growing up as a
Christian there was a bit out of the
ordinary.

From my earliest days, I was surrounded by Buddhists, Hindus, and Muslims. When I was young, I had friends who couldn't attend my birthday parties because they had to go with their family to burn incense at their grandfather's grave—an annual tradition for many Buddhists. In high school, I worked part-time as a copywriter for a small ad agency, and my fellow copywriters were Muslims. Conversations with my colleagues occasionally turned to matters of faith, and we talked about our different views of life with very little awkwardness.

My dad was raised in a Hindu family. His father was an official or elder at the local Hindu temple, and during most of his growing-up years, my dad wanted to follow in his father's footsteps.

Then he met my mom. They were both students at the University of Singapore; he was majoring in political science, and she was a social science major. My mom had grown up in the Anglican Church—a contribution of the good Brits who had colonized Malaysia—but her faith was nominal at best.

As my parents' relationship grew more serious, my mom drew a line in the sand. She made it clear that she would only marry a Christian. My father wasted no time in converting to Christianity, a decision that forever changed the way his family interacted with him. From that point on, he and my mom were cut off from all but the most basic, formal communications with his parents and many of his siblings. Changing religions in Malaysia is not something that people do all that often. Rejecting the faith of your family is a slap in the face that blatantly dishonors your parents and ancestors.

WHEN I DREAMED OF AFRICA

Growing up in a Christian home, I got saved about 352 times before my eighth birthday. Every time someone at church talked about heaven and hell, I would think, *I don't want to go to hell. It sounds awful. But what if I've done something recently that has somehow canceled my passport to heaven? I don't want to take the chance. I'm going to say the prayer again.* And before I knew it, my feet were leading me toward that familiar spot at the altar. I think I responded to every altar call they had, and most of my "conversions" were in response to the old line, "If you got hit by a truck today, do you know where you would go?" That one got me every time. Maybe you can relate.

One year, my parents sent me to a church-sponsored children's camp about fifty kilometers from home, high up in the rolling hills of Malaysia. I was there with a few hundred other city kids, all of us getting our first taste of being away from home and out in the wild.

It was there I found my destiny in the eyes of an American lady.

She was a missionary who had come to Malaysia to work with young children. And we were a roomful of young Asian kids. We had finished singing and were starting to get restless as we sat down on rattan mats laid out on the concrete floor. Outside the windows was a sea of rich, green foliage. The sun was setting and the tropical insects were tuning up for the evening. Ceiling fans spun noisily overhead, accomplishing little more than wrapping the thick, humid air around us like a giant, damp towel.

The American lady walked to the front, and almost

immediately, like a lullaby sung to a baby, her voice settled the room. She had a way of making us listen. Every
word was like a gentle tide washing against the shore.
Her face was delicately wrinkled, her smile was calm,
and there was a gentle magic in her eyes. In my memory,
she was a cross between Princess Diana and Mother
Teresa, but maybe that's because it was the early 1980s
and she was one of the very few Americans I had met.
Whatever it was, I listened with rapt attention as she
told us a story about the explorer Dr. David Livingstone.

It wasn't your average Sunday school lesson—there
was no flannel board, no props—but we were captivated. The missionary told us that Dr. Livingstone
knew at an early age that he wanted to venture into
unknown parts of the world to tell people about Jesus.
She talked about how he became a doctor and went to
Africa to help the people there. We were mesmerized as
she described the impact he had as an explorer and as
a missionary. He charted new territory and preached to
people who had not heard about Jesus.

The room was as still as a stone—and remember,
there were a couple hundred kids there. The sounds of
the forest had long since faded into the background. All
we heard was the American lady's small, hushed voice,
which cracked gently as she told us how Dr. Livingstone
had died, and how his body was buried in England but
his heart remained in Africa. As I watched her eyes brim
up with tears, my own eyes began to overflow. I could
not control it.

We started singing again, a quiet song. The
American lady was still standing in front, asking us to
pray about giving our lives to be used by God, to be

> *I wanted my life to count toward something far greater than myself. This was what God was asking us to do.*

part of something extraordinary. For me, there was no decision—it was obvious. How could I do anything less than be involved somehow in changing people's lives? I wanted my life to count toward something far greater than myself. This was what God was asking us to do. This was what David Livingstone and the American lady had given their lives to accomplish. Why would I choose anything different?

EXPANDING MY VISION

Throughout my childhood, my parents fed my love of books. I looked forward to going to the bookstore to see what new delight my weekly allowance would afford. Every Saturday, after a morning swim, we went to the library and spent the afternoon hours reading. Then the whole family would gather over dinner and discuss what we had read. Our dinner conversations were about social issues, faith, the Bible, our friends. My sister and I grew up with a very big picture of the world.

On my tenth birthday, my parents gave me the autobiography of George Mueller, a man who had changed the lives of more than 100,000 children by building orphanages in Bristol, England during the 1800s. I was hooked. From then on, I couldn't get my hands on such books fast enough. I wanted to read about people who had made a significant impact on the world. I read about Charles Finney, John Wesley, and an intercessor named Rees Howells. I threw in an occasional Hardy Boys mystery, but for the most part, I devoured stories about people worth remembering.

"THE LORD HAS SUCH GREAT THINGS FOR YOU"

My dream of one day doing something significant was further fueled by the people around me as I grew up. At our church, sweet, middle-aged women would come up to me on Sunday mornings and say, "Oh, Glenn, the Lord has such great things for you" or "The Lord wants to do great things in your life" or "The Lord is going to use you in mighty ways."

As I got older, I discovered that those phrases were simply a Christian version of "Atta boy" or "Go get 'em, Tiger." Even so, it affected my attitude and expectations. Every word was like fresh blood rushing into my young heart. I knew it was true: I was destined for greatness.

When I got to college, I found that many of my friends had grown up on a steady diet of similar lines. The more we talked, the more I realized that we didn't simply have dreams, we had *destiny*. Never had I been surrounded by so many people with such grand and inevitable futures! Now we were all sitting around waiting for something great to happen to us.

The thing about vision is that sometimes we get a bigger picture than we can handle all at one time. Sometimes, God gives us a glimpse of the possibilities, but it isn't all for right now. But because of that, we make the mistake of thinking that none of it is for right

The more we talked, the more I realized that we didn't simply have dreams, we had destiny. . . . Now we were all sitting around waiting for something great to happen to us.

now. We act as if the mere possession of a dream is the end of our responsibility. We say quietly to ourselves, "All my life people have told me that I'm going to be involved in great things. I've been reading and hearing about people who really made a difference with their lives. So, okay, I'm ready for some great things to happen. Here I go. I'm waiting for great things. The Lord is going to do great things in my life, and I'm just going to wait for this dream to become a reality."

LIFE ON TIVO

As a result of our great expectations, we sort of TiVo'd our lives without really intending to—just hit "pause" and put everything on hold. In effect, each of us was saying, "I know that God wants to use me to accomplish great things. So I'm going to store up all the greatness that's building in me right now, and then one day I'll find myself in an arena before thousands and thousands of people, and then—*BAM!*—I'll release all that greatness on everyone."

Well, maybe no one would have said it quite that way, but here's how I knew that some of my peers thought that way. In my theology classes, many of the students were on track to become pastors and leaders in churches across the country or around the world. But they were only *planning* for it. In the meantime, while they were getting all their theology and learning all their ministry techniques, they were not serving in any local church or ministry. For that matter, some weren't even attending a church. (Shhhh! Don't tell the R.A.!) They weren't a part of any small or local change while they were in school. They were just studying and storing up greatness.

That seemed a little odd to me, because God's not going to say, when you graduate from college, "Oh, wow! You finished your bachelor's or your master's in theology. Fantastic! Here's a traveling ministry to thousands of people every weekend." Or, "Here's a church that you're going to grow to national prominence."

We can't bottle up our passion, energy, and dreams of action until we're on the right stage. . . . If we try to save our vision for the perfect day, we'll lose it.

The problem with storing up greatness is . . . well, it's impossible. We can't bottle up our passion, energy, and dreams of action until we're on the right stage. If we try, we will get there only to find that all the greatness has leaked out. If we try to save our vision for the perfect day, we'll lose it. We'll get to the place where we think that we're ready and find that we have nothing left to give.

If we live each phase of life as if it's a stepping-stone to greatness, we will find ourselves living each moment at half-speed. God wants us to take what's stirring in our hearts *today* and act on it here and now. Instead of waiting for great things to happen, we should be asking God, "What do I do about this idea *now?* I know that someday there may be a greater fulfillment of the dream—maybe there's a piece that won't unfold until twenty years from now—but what do I do here and now?" Everything that God has put inside us must be expressed and acted on here and now—or it will never multiply and grow. No matter how small and seemingly insignificant it might be, we can do *something* today; we can get started with *something*.

THE ONE BIG THING

I work with college-age students at our church, and many of them have big dreams in their hearts, but they feel as if they're in a holding pattern, and they're kind of embarrassed about their situation in life. It isn't so much that they're trying to store up greatness; they just haven't yet figured out where to start.

I heard a comedian once talk about the difference between university students and students at a community college. He said if you ever ask somebody what school they go to and it's a university, the answer is really easy. "I go to the University of Colorado," or "I go to USC" or "NYU" or whatever it is. Short and sweet. But if you ask a community college student the same question, the answer is always quite a bit longer.

"Oh, well, I'm just trying to . . . see, they messed up my transcript and I'm just working on getting some financial aid right now. . . . Eventually I'm going to transfer to . . ." and it just goes on and on, because they're embarrassed about not feeling as if they're "on track," whatever that means.

I find the same situation with a lot of people who are out of school but haven't yet found "the one big thing" to devote their lives to. They say, "Yeah, I'm doing this now. . . . I work at Starbucks now, but eventually I'll work for a Christian publisher, or a big church, or I'll go on the mission field, or eventually I'll get to the place where I'm doing great things for God."

As I've thought this through and talked to many different young people, and even wrestled with this tension in my own life, I've come to realize that there isn't some point where all of a sudden we reach greatness or we get to do great things. I think we have the possibility of being a part of great things *every day* and maybe not even know it. As the biblical character Jacob discovered when he encamped at Bethel and encountered the "stairway to heaven" in a dream, "Surely the Lord is in this place, and I wasn't even aware of it!"[1] Just as surely, God is working through our lives right where we are today—in those conversations at the water fountain, or over lunch, or whatever situation we're in. Surely God is in those places, even if we don't realize it. The "greatness" isn't always obvious. It is often so sublime that we simply miss it.

We all too easily *assume* that the place of significance is someplace else. Overseas. On the mission field. Just around the next bend. When we turn forty. When we make our first million. Wherever. And we don't even consider that lasting change begins right where we are. We don't consider the possibility that God can use us right here and now. We don't seriously consider that God has us right where we are for a very good reason. He can use us here. If God can use us anywhere, why do we assume that where he wants to use us is someplace other than where we are right now? Think about it. What are the things that are right in front of you, right now, that you're overlooking because you've set your sights elsewhere? Who are the people you've ignored because they're not the remote tribe you've set your heart on reaching? Why not start by looking for a small, local opportunity to serve and to do some good? Open your eyes. Listen more closely to others. Take that initial small step, that simple act of obedience, and see what comes of it.

> *Nehemiah was just an ordinary man who ended up making an extraordinary difference.*

OUT OF THE ORDINARY . . .

One of my favorite stories in the Bible is the story of Nehemiah. I'm drawn to Nehemiah because, like many characters in the Bible, he made a significant impact on history. But unlike our other biblical heroes who are kings or prophets or priests—or the Son of God himself—Nehemiah was just an ordinary man who ended up making an extraordinary difference. He was not one of the twelve disciples. As far as we know, not one miracle happened through Nehemiah's life. He didn't utter a single prophetic word, heal anyone, or win a decisive battle. He was a cupbearer, and he became most famous for his role as a contractor. Not your average Bible action hero. Still, he stands apart in my mind precisely because of his averageness. I love Nehemiah's story because, despite his humble beginnings, he finds himself in the middle of a moment that changes history.

Born a Jew in a foreign country, Nehemiah was a child of what was known as the Dispersion. More than a century earlier, his Jewish ancestors had been taken captive by the Babylonians as punishment for disobeying God. When the Persians later overran the Babylonians, many of the Jews were moved on to Persia. That's where Nehemiah was born, and he knew no other home than Susa, the capital city. Yet he was never quite at home there.

He had heard the stories of how God had promised to make Abraham a great nation and gave him a son in his old age; of how God sent Moses to deliver Abraham's descendents when they were large in number and enslaved by the mighty Egyptians; how an entire generation died in the desert of Sinai because of their lack of faith; how Joshua had led a new generation in victory over army after army as they took the land; how God gave Israel the great king David, and how every king thereafter was measured against him. He had heard about the prophecies that foretold the exile, and also the promise of a return to Judah, when God would bring the people back to the land as proof of his unending faithfulness. Now, in Nehemiah's lifetime, the promised return was beginning to occur.

Certainly, Nehemiah's situation incited questions about his identity, about his heritage, and about his true home. He'd grown up in a culture that questioned God's sovereignty and justice. He'd grown up in a culture of doubt, where uncertainty was the only thing that made sense. It was not so different from our own culture in that regard. Yet somehow Nehemiah clung to the stories of home. He grew up longing for a land he'd never seen, and hoping for a city he'd only heard about. He grew up believing in redemption and trusting in a God who seemed distant. Somehow, amid all the confusion and questioning, Nehemiah found a spark of faith and fanned it into a burning flame.

> *Yet somehow Nehemiah clung to the stories of home. He grew up longing for a land he'd never seen, and hoping for a city he'd only heard about.*

It's hard to say whether Nehemiah had a sense of the world-changing importance of what he was about to do, but I suspect he didn't. When his moment came, he didn't set out to change the world; he was just doing the necessary thing, the one thing he could do that needed to be done. But regardless of whether Nehemiah had a sense of what he would accomplish, I think we can glean from his story some life-changing principles that will influence our own stories.

In the opening scene of the book of Nehemiah, we find that one of Nehemiah's brothers, Hanani, has returned from a visit to Judah. Apparently, the Persians had allowed some of the Jews to return from captivity to their native land, and Hanani was among a group that had come back to Susa to give a report. When Nehemiah asked how things were going in Judah, Hanani replied, "It's bad, Nehemiah. Bad. The walls are burned. The stones are . . . it's just rubble. It's all in a pile . . . it's ground zero, man. It's just a mess."[2]

The few Jews who had returned to Jerusalem were living in dire circumstances. The walls of the city lay in ruins, open to every kind of danger. The gates had been burned beyond repair. The desolation left the city exposed to the elements, overgrown, and looted. The city of God was a dead locust of a town, a crushed shell.

When Nehemiah heard the news, he sat down and wept. Though he had never been to his homeland, he knew that Jerusalem was the pride of the nation. It was the capital city, and it was destroyed. He was so overwhelmed with grief that he fasted and prayed for several days, confessing his own sins, the sins of his family and of his people, the Jews. As he prayed, he reminded God of some earlier promises made to the people of Israel:

> Please remember what you told your servant Moses:
> "If you are unfaithful to me, I will scatter you among

the nations. But if you return to me and obey my
commands and live by them, then even if you are
exiled to the ends of the earth, I will bring you back
to the place I have chosen for my name to be
honored."[3]

Nehemiah decided that he must go to Jerusalem and do
something about the condition of the city. He prayed
that God would grant him favor with the Persian king,
and that the king would grant his request. Nehemiah's
love for Jerusalem would not let him stand by and simply wait for something great to happen.

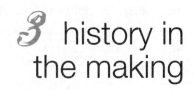

$\mathcal{3}$ history in the making

In 1963, MIT meteorologist
Edward Lorenz encountered some
unexpected results while running a
computerized weather simulation to study
how air currents rise and fall when heated
by the sun. At one point in the experiment, Lorenz restarted the simulation
in order to review the data he was
getting. He entered the same initial
values, expecting to get identical
results. Instead, the results were

markedly different. It didn't make sense. After rerunning the experiment several more times, Lorenz discovered a slight discrepancy in his initial values.

The numbers Lorenz had used were accurate to three decimal places, but the computer was calculating the numbers to six decimal places. The deviation seemed insignificant, yet it had a profound effect on the consistency of the results. Lorenz then realized that his experiment was demonstrating a property of physics known as "sensitivity to initial conditions," first identified by the nineteenth century French mathematician Henri Poincaré. Poincaré suggested that "small differences in the initial positions may lead to enormous differences in the final phenomena."[1] In other words, small changes at the beginning can lead to big differences at the end.

If a butterfly flaps its wings in Brazil, does it cause a tornado in Texas?

Lorenz applied this principle to the science of weather forecasting and hypothesized that small localized changes could initiate a chain reaction of weather patterns that would have far-reaching effects. To make his point, he posed the somewhat whimsical question, "If a butterfly flaps its wings in Brazil, does it cause a tornado in Texas?" Thus, the phenomenon of big differences resulting from small changes came to be known as "the butterfly effect."

Even if Lorenz's question isn't literal, it is nonetheless interesting. A butterfly flapping its wings is a humble, fragile, small, and seemingly insignificant act. It's also a necessary act. Flapping its wings is what a butterfly does to get from one place to the next. Yet it is possible that through a series of interrelated consequences, the small, local act of wing-flapping gradually culminates in a raging Texas tornado.

Like Lorenz's hypothetical butterfly in Brazil, our efforts to create lasting change often have humble beginnings. Actually, sometimes we don't even realize that we're beginning anything all that special! Those who change the world are not always those who set out to. They're simply being faithful with the small, necessary things right where we are. And somehow, over a long period of time, it ends up making a world of difference.

Of course, the butterfly effect is just a hypothesis. It's not a rock-solid, scientific truth. Life doesn't always turn out like the recipe says—actually, neither does my cooking! This book is not a step-by-step guide to changing the world. There are no formulas, but there are principles. There are common scenes in the events that have shaped our world—common characteristics, a common path, by which lasting change takes place. We can trace the footprints of those who changed history for the better, and learn from those who made their lives count for something beyond themselves. This book is simply a collection of those principles, an unpacking of those big ideas seen in the Bible—God's account of history—and confirmed by our own records of human history.

We can trace the footprints of those who changed history for the better, and learn from those who made their lives count for something beyond themselves.

OUR PLACE IN HISTORY

I have to confess something: I am a certified history nerd. I actually read the textbook for my humanities classes in college. I never slept through a single video lecture—not even the ones where Francis Schaeffer was wearing really long socks. I love reading stories of past accomplishments and looking for ways to connect them to contemporary culture. I enjoy mining for timeless principles in the exploits of people from the past, and applying those principles to life today and making history now.

As much as we may think that our day and age is unique in human history—and in many ways it is—there's also a sense in which there's nothing new under the sun. When it comes to human nature, human activities, and the creation of lasting change, the same principles apply today that have applied down through the ages. But before we can apply those principles to make some history of our own, we need to answer a very important question: How is history made? Is it an irresistible force that moves us along, a tide that simply carries us away? Or is it a malleable work-in-progress that human beings shape for themselves? Do we achieve greatness, or is greatness thrust upon us? Who is in control? Is it fate, chance? Is it us? Is it God?

As a Christian, I believe that God is the creator of all things, and he is ultimately in control. But that doesn't really answer our question. As humans, we are not passive pawns that God shifts and shuttles in a purely deterministic game of chess. Our lives are part of a bigger story, and somehow our choices contribute to it. We have a purpose, but we are not puppets. Part of our life's journey is to learn how to surrender to God and cooperate with him in shaping our lives around his purpose. Saying that God is sovereign means acknowledging that the story is his, and it's about him. It also means recognizing that he has allowed us to participate in the story with him. He's the author and finisher, but we have very important roles to play.

GOD AT THE IMPROV

Think of it this way: Human history is like an improvisational *movie*—that's right, not an improv sketch, an entire movie—with God as the writer, director, producer, and lead actor. It's a work in progress, and we, the other improv actors, have the opportunity to put in a few scenes of our own. We're not just extras in a busy boulevard scene; we're characters with unique parts, personalities, and idiosyncrasies.

So let's imagine a scene. You're on a date. Let's say it's your first date in a while—you were taking a break from the dating scene, you know, taking some time to clear your head and reconnect with God. In this scene, there are a few things you know the director doesn't want—you can't be a jerk; you can't end up in bed together, you know the limits—but the restaurant, the activity, the conversation, that's all you.

Like a good actor, God leads you in each scene with subtle cues and actions.

Now, as it turns out, God is also in that scene. You soon discover he's in every scene, though you don't always see him. As you try your hand at this edgy style of acting called improv, you see that God improvises right along with you. And like a good actor, he leads you in each scene with subtle cues and actions. In case you forget the overall story, he's there to help you not ruin the picture, and to find your way back to the plot. God never forgets; he wrote the synopsis, remember?

The direction you go with the evening is your choice: You either advance the plot of God's story, or you digress and distract from it. That's why you can't end up in bed with your date: It's outside the plot and would sidetrack the story that God is trying to tell through you. If you allow your scenes to be hijacked by sin, they'll end up on the cutting room floor, because they'll be ruined. But when you let God redeem your life, it can become a great scene, displaying a powerful performance by the main character.

God's brilliance is seen in his ability to work the various parts and players together into a larger story that serves his ultimate purpose. He knows what each scene is for and what purpose it serves in the overall

God's brilliance is seen in his ability to work the various parts and players together into a larger story that serves his ultimate purpose.

picture. Still, how each scene unfolds depends in part on how the players play it. We can make choices that take a scene in a direction that God did not intend, but when we do that, we hinder the development of the story and don't advance the plot. (If you've ever been to an improv performance and suffered through a sketch that just doesn't work, you know what I'm talking about. It makes it awkward for everyone.) When we take a scene away from the storyline that God has prepared, our actions in that scene become pointless because God won't use them in the final cut. Although God can use even our "cutting room floor" scenes to refine our character and teach us important lessons, the more we come to understand the roles he has given us to play, the more our lives can become a part of the story God is ultimately trying to tell. The good news is, he's on the scene, always leading us back to the story. After all, he's the star. The story is his.

GOD ENTERS THE SCENE

God loves breaking into history. He is not content merely to observe from a distance. He did not set the world up to run like clockwork while he sat back and watched time tick by. When humans, the crown of his creation, derailed the original story, God didn't wring his hands and wonder what to do about it. Instead, he chose to solve the problem by inserting himself into the scene. The Son of God wrapped himself in human flesh, and was born as a carpenter's son. His birth was announced by angels and surrounded by barn animals. Within the first few years of his life, he was adored by wealthy kings and rogue shepherds. He came to save self-righteous God-followers and shamed sinners alike. He was completely God and yet all man.

The mystery of the Incarnation—and our difficulty explaining it—lies in this uncorrupted combination of divinity and humanity. Jesus Christ, Son of God and Son of Man, is God's answer to the human condition, the rescue from our otherwise inescapable demise. Our savior, if there were to be one, had to be divine in order to be perfect and without sin, and thus capable of appeasing the wrath of God. But this savior also had to be human, because it was humankind's wrongs he would pay for, and our place that he would have to take.

The Incarnation was the perfect answer. Divinity joined with humanity was the only way to satisfy God's justice and also display his love. God supplied our salvation by sending Jesus Christ to earth to live a sinless life, die a sacrificial death on our behalf, rise again on the third day, and ascend into heaven. The Incarnation is absolutely central to our salvation.

The Incarnation is also an unmistakable clue to how God works. It is our clearest insight into God's modus operandi. So, let's make two crucial observations. First, God is not a passive observer of human history. But neither is he the puppet master of the universe. He loves to lead us from inside the story; he shapes history by taking an active role in it, while at the same time standing outside of it. (It's weird, I know; but he's God. He can have his cake and eat it too.)

> *God loves to lead us from inside the story; he shapes history by taking an active role in it, while at the same time standing outside of it.*

Secondly, God works in both the dramatic and the prosaic—sometimes in the same instance. Consider again the birth of Jesus. On the one hand, the heavens were lit by singing angels and brilliant stars. On the other hand, the helpless infant lay in a manger at the back of an obscure, overcrowded, small town inn—not a Roman palace or even a courtyard in Jerusalem. God's most noteworthy entrance onto the world's stage was simultaneously dramatic and prosaic.

It would seem difficult for most followers of Christ to miss his most dramatic moments. Yet those closest to him during his time on earth seemed to make "missing it" an art form. (Not that we've necessarily done much better in our own day and age.) They missed the punch line of many of his parables and stories; they didn't realize who the most important people in the kingdom of heaven were (children, in their innocence); and they missed the central point of his life (death and resurrection, not political ascendancy).

This arresting combination of the unmistakably supernatural and the unremarkably ordinary is the surest mark of God's activity. While we spend time searching for God in heaven's clouds, he roams the earth with dirt under his fingernails and shadows under his eyes. Our Savior is one who callused his hands swinging a hammer and an ax. He used dust and spit to heal a blind man. God's method has always been to wrap the supernatural in flesh and blood. He works through human beings inside space and time. He shows up in the most ordinary scenes, the kinds of scenes where we don't necessarily have our Handycam rolling.

My wife and I have two little girls who are absolutely adorable. They got my skin tone and my wife's good looks. I'm already dreading their high school years! As my elder daughter, Sophia, approaches two, I'm witnessing firsthand the truth of that phrase so often repeated among parents: "They just grow up so fast!" So, we've been trying to capture on camera as many moments as we can. So far all the moments we have on tape are all the moments you might expect: Sophia rolling over, her stumbling first steps, her first birthday party, and so on. But the moments I wish I could relive are all the ones that came with no warning—the sudden, spontaneous giggles, the shy look on her face when she tries to play hide and seek, the hilarious phrases she pulls out of the air, the random fits of "dancing." Those are the things I wish I could catch on film.

Several weeks ago, Sophia got an ear infection and a really high fever. It was her first truly miserable ailment.

She lost her appetite, moped around the house, and clung to me like an obsessive ex-girlfriend. For some reason, she didn't want anyone else—not her grandparents or her aunt and uncle who were all visiting from out of town, and not even her mother. She wanted Daddy to hold her, Daddy to rock her, Daddy to read to her, and Daddy to wake up with her every few hours in the middle of the night several nights in a row. As exhausting as it was, those days were some of my favorite days so far as a dad. Sophia and I bonded in a very special way. It seemed as if for the first time, her father could provide something she needed. I remember lying down beside her watching her fall asleep in my arms and feeling such an amazing sense of fullness, of meaning. I remember thinking, *I am a father. What did I do to deserve this beautiful gift? This is what life is all about!* In those moments, I forgot about the stress of work or how tired I was. I sensed God himself surrounding me. And right then I wished I had my Handycam rolling.

LUNCHBOX MIRACLES

God is there in our non-Handycam moments. We can offer him the most mundane moments, the dullest scenes or routines and watch him do a miracle, just as Jesus did with the five loaves and two fish offered by a young boy. Jesus took the boy's meager lunch, blessed it, broke it, and supernaturally multiplied it to feed thousands. He took the ordinary and made it extraordinary. In his hands, the mundane became miraculous.

It's up to us to recognize that God is still at work in our scenes. He's asking us to surrender our meager lunches—the common, necessary stuff of everyday life—to him. In so doing, we live out the Incarnation and bring God to earth. We become participants in the mysterious model of the unmistakably supernatural in the midst of the common and mundane. We become carriers of the divine amid the broken humans around us. The difference between Christians and non-Christians is that the non-Christians have only their humanity to fall back on; frailty defines their entire existence. But for those who believe in Christ and are born again—they become "partakers of the divine nature," active participants in God's glorious mystery, having "escaped the corruption that is in the world."[2] That is the Christian's distinguishing mark.

To be conduits of change, we must be faithful stewards of the small, ordinary moments.

To be conduits of change, we must be faithful stewards of the small, ordinary moments. God does not need us to be supernatural or mystical; that's what he is. He needs us to be human, common, and earthy. We are the vessels of clay; he is the exceedingly great treasure.

Just as the point of Christ's life was not his ascension but his incarnation, our goal as human beings on earth is not to escape earth and ascend to heaven, but to let heaven, through us, invade the earth we occupy. Every scene becomes significant as we find God there. And every scene is thus brought under his direction.

When we've done our parts, when we've faithfully

played the roles assigned to us, we'll find our names in the closing credits, and our parts described as "Good and Faithful Servants."

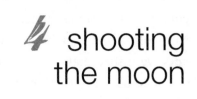

4 shooting the moon

I was ten years old when my family first moved to America. My parents had decided that God was calling them into full-time Christian ministry and they needed to get some Bible training. So we moved to Portland, Oregon, for three years.

After returning to Malaysia, my parents spent the next four years serving on the pastoral staff of a large church in Kuala Lumpur, the capital city, while I completed my high school education through an American homeschool curriculum. (I would have been completely lost if I had attempted to return to the Malay-language public schools.) I spent my days hanging out at the church and their newly founded Bible college, of which my parents were now in charge. I did my homework in the library, sat in on a few Old Testament history classes, and grabbed lunch with my dad and some of the students and pastors.

When it was time for me to return to the States for college, we started packing as only good Asians can. We dug up a good, sturdy suitcase made from some sort of synthetic material and large enough to fit most of my cousins. Then came the task of finding suitable clothes. None of us had ever been to Oklahoma, but my parents were sure that the winters would be cold and that I needed as many turtlenecks as possible. So the Great Clothing Drive commenced. From aunts and uncles in Canada, from friends who had lived in cold climates, and from kind church acquaintances who once had visited the U.S., came sweaters, coats, ski pants, winter boots, thermal socks, long johns, Russian snow hats, and wooly earmuffs. And then there were trips to the mall, trying to find dressy clothes on a budget. (We were sure that American college students dressed up to go to class. Because I went to a private Christian university, we were at least partially correct.) Remember, though, that I hadn't been in the States for four years. The last time I was there, rayon shirts with crazy-colored prints and bolo ties were in.

So you can imagine what I looked like when I first met Holly, the wonderful woman who is now my wife.

I was working at the college library and barely had enough money for an occasional meal out or maybe a Wal-Mart run for Totino's pizza. I had no car, no computer, and no real sense of style. (I once came down to the lobby of our dorm in a pair of silk boxers, because I had no idea that boxer shorts were not a new style of short pants but rather were to be worn underneath pants.) I wore gold-rimmed, oval-shaped glasses, and had hair cropped so close to my head that my earlobes looked like they were ready to carry me off in the Oklahoma wind.

I was a junior and Holly was a freshman. I was struck by the beauty of her wholly American appeal. She might have been struck by my favorite multicolored sweater, with swirls and triangles that would have made Bill Cosby jealous. Or maybe it was my puffy, pink wind jacket with gold and blue trim. (Both outfits eventually made their way into date pictures with Holly and then later to the thrift store.)

Before long, I was engaged in all sorts of foolishness to express my love for Holly and to try to win her heart.

At any rate, we met through mutual friends. I guessed her to be a cheerleader from California, and she probably guessed me to be a sweet nerd from another country. As it turned out, she was a farm girl from Iowa, and I was . . .

well . . . a sweet nerd from another country. We began to talk and got better acquainted at a friend's ballroom dancing birthday party. The group hangouts led to one-on-one conversations at the cafeteria, and eventually to dates. Before long, I was engaged in all sorts of foolishness to express my love for her and to try to win her heart.

As we started dating, I realized that the key to winning her over for good was first to win her family, especially her grandparents. While spending a few days with her extended family over a Christmas break, I quickly discovered the secret to my desired success: card games. Now, I grew up playing cards occasionally with my family and developed some decent skills, but my in-laws are card-playing fiends. Maybe it's those long, cold Iowa winters. Or maybe it's something in the water. But whatever the reason, I'm convinced that Midwesterners have developed a superior card-playing gene.

At any rate, because I don't hunt, fish, or play horseshoes very well, proving my card-playing ability seemed to be my only hope of securing the admiration and approval of Holly's sweet and classically Midwestern grandparents. As the only Malaysian her family had ever met, I felt I desperately needed to impress them.

Of all the games they played, I saw my best chance to win with Hearts. If you've ever played, you know that points are a bad thing in that game. Every heart counts as a point, and the queen of spades counts for thirteen. However, if you can nab *all* the hearts and the dreaded queen of spades, the tables are turned and you can stick your opponents with twenty-six points. This go-for-broke strategy is called "shooting the moon." Naturally, it seemed like the best way for me to impress Holly's family. I thought, *If I could just shoot the moon, they would surely stand in awe!*

So, of course I tried it on every hand. And then, it happened. Early in the game, I succeeded in shooting the moon. My acceptance was certain! Their admiration for me would spring up like a bountiful corn harvest.

But something odd happened to me. I wasn't satisfied. I needed to shoot the moon again. *Surely they won't suspect it again.* I became so fixated on trying to shoot the moon on every remaining hand, that I actually gathered so many unwanted points by coming close but failing that I lost the game. Shooting the moon and losing the game. It takes a special talent to do that in Hearts!

SMALL CHANGE

God's way of shaping history is not to shoot the moon. But that is so often our MO. When we see a problem, our impulse is to fix it as quickly and easily as possible. If it's a big problem, we're tempted to look for a big solution. We want to fix things with an overly dramatic, knee-jerk response. Low on cash and worried about your financial future? A lottery ticket might be just the

> *When we see a problem, our impulse is to fix it as quickly and easily as possible. If it's a big problem, we're tempted to look for a big solution.*

thing. Pants feeling a little too tight? Skipping dinner for a week is the way to go.

Coming up with a "shoot the moon" strategy for every game, every problem, or every goal we have in life is the surest way to live in frustration. There is no quick road to greatness, no shortcut to changing the world. When we insist on looking for those shortcuts, we end up squandering the good opportunities we have, the small, ordinary opportunities that come without glory or excitement. They are the weak things that the strong are too proud to try. They are the foolish things that the wise consider beneath them. They are small actions, simple opportunities, but we squander them because they don't have the rewards, the prestige, or the respect that we want.

No, creating lasting change is not about shooting the moon. Making a difference has nothing to do with impassioned speeches or million man marches. It's not about starting a revolution or spending billions of dollars. Those are dramatic spectacles that do not create long-term change; they're here and gone. If you gave it all away yesterday, suddenly you have nothing to give today.

> *Making a difference has nothing to do with impassioned speeches or million man marches. It's not about starting a revolution or spending billions of dollars.*

What we're really after is lasting change, not flashes in the pan. The kind of change worth recording in history is the kind that endures long after we're gone. And that kind of change is often the consequence of small actions. That's the first secret of creating lasting change: Change is small.

A LITTLE PIECE OF TAPE

Sometimes it's the smallest things that make the biggest difference. Not sure if you believe that? Just ask Frank Wills.

Frank was a security guard, a profession more often known for its slouches than its heroes. But Frank was no slouch. One night, as he was making his rounds in the office building where he worked, he found a piece of tape on the latch of a door to the basement, keeping it unlocked. Perhaps someone had needed quick, hands-free access through the door and had used the tape for a temporary aid. It could have been a janitor, or a lawyer carrying some case files out to her car. Whatever the case, it was long past office hours, so Frank removed the tape and continued on his rounds.

An hour later, he returned to the basement door and found a new piece of tape stuck over the latch. Now he was suspicious. He immediately called the police. An unmarked cruiser pulled up outside the building so as not to disrupt the intruders if they were still there. It didn't take long for the police to find the five burglars, crouching behind desks in an office. And it didn't take long for this little break-in to escalate into a problem of national proportions.

You see, Frank Wills was a security guard at the headquarters of the Democratic National Committee—in the Watergate Building in Washington, D.C. The five men arrested that night were found to have White House connections. A Senate committee was formed to investigate, and President Richard Nixon and several of his top aides were eventually implicated. Under the shadow of impeachment, Nixon resigned, a little more than two years after Frank Wills discovered the little piece of tape.

What makes this story incredible to me is not that Wills found the tape stuck to the latch; he had little to do with that. Almost any other security guard would have noticed it. What makes Frank Wills exceptional to me is that he came back to check on the door again. It was the second piece of tape that tipped him off. He didn't have to go back and check the door; he had found the first piece of tape and removed it. He could have dismissed it, explained it, excused it. But he went back. Something as simple as making an extra round, something as small as a piece of tape, affected forever the legacy of the president of the United States of America.

As a twenty-four-year-old, Frank Wills may have had some dreams, but he certainly wasn't intending to shape history with his job. He was a security guard. He knew he would probably never run for office or earn millions of dollars. In fact, he lived in poverty most of his life. He patrolled an empty building night after night. He never tried to shoot the moon. But Frank Wills did his job well.

Lasting change is often the result of simple faithfulness with something that seems inconsequential. A big impact usually begins with a small act. For Frank Wills, it was about making a second round through the

> *Lasting change is often the result of simple faithfulness with something that seems inconsequential. A big impact usually begins with a small act.*

building. If we're serious about making a difference and creating lasting change, we need to learn faithfulness and excellence in the little things. Maybe then we'll quit talking about shooting the moon—that shortcut to greatness—and learn to play our cards correctly. Change, after all, starts by doing small things well.

THE HERO THAT ALMOST WAS

Sometimes doing the small things means simply staying awake. When Jesus was nearing the end of his earthly life, he urged his disciples to remain faithful and alert.

> Be on guard, keep awake. For you do not know when the time will come. It is like a man going on a journey, when he leaves home and puts his servants in charge, each with his work, and commands the doorkeeper to stay awake. Therefore stay awake— for you do not know when the master of the house will come, in the evening, or at midnight, or when the cock crows, or in the morning—lest he come suddenly and find you asleep. And what I say to you I say to all: Stay awake.[1]

Cyril Evans learned this lesson the hard way.

Evans was a radio operator aboard the British steam-ship *Californian,* under the command of Captain Stanley Lord. The *Californian* embarked from England on April 5, 1912, bound for Boston. Though the ship could carry as many as forty-seven passengers and fifty-five crew-men, on that particular voyage, there were no passengers on board. Nine days into the journey, they encountered a large and dangerous ice field just south of Newfoundland. Deciding it was too dangerous to continue, the *Californian* reversed its engines and stopped for the night.

Around midnight, the officers on watch spotted another ship in the distance. Curious to know who else was out in the middle of the ice field, they tried to estab-lish contact by flashing their Morse lamp. But there was no response.

Suddenly, an explosion of white light filled the night sky. It seemed to come from the direction of the other ship. It was followed by another white flash. And then another. In all, five rockets exploded in the distance. The officers decided to inform Captain Lord of this pecu-liar occurrence. The captain asked whether the rockets were a company signal, but the officers on watch weren't sure. Lord instructed them to keep trying to contact the ship with the Morse lamp, but only to inform him if anything changed.

The officers continued to flash the beacon light, hop-ing for some sort of response. But none was received. Instead, the cabin lights of the distant ship seemed to be disappearing, as if the ship were leaving. Around 1:40 a.m., they saw a final explosion of white light, and by 2:00 a.m., the cabin lights were out of sight.

When Captain Lord awoke, sometime after four o'clock on the morning of April 15, he went out to the bridge to determine how the *Californian* would navigate through the ice. Around 6:00 a.m., when Cyril Evans returned to his post in the radio room, the crew of the *Californian* heard the shocking news: The RMS *Titanic* had sunk overnight.

There is some disagreement over the precise proximity of the *Californian* to the *Titanic*. Some estimate that the distance was as close as eight or nine miles. Others say it was more like nineteen miles. But either way, they were close enough to have helped. Instead, the first ship on the scene was the *Carpathia,* which had steamed from fifty-eight miles away when first informed of the *Titanic*'s situation shortly after midnight.

Captain Lord of the *Californian* was later criticized by British and American investigators of the tragedy for his inaction. After all, why hadn't anyone tried to make radio contact with the *Titanic*? Where was Cyril Evans?

As it turned out, Evans had contacted the *Titanic* on the evening of the fourteenth, shortly before the ship struck the iceberg. Around 11:00 p.m., Evans, Captain Lord, and a few officers had spotted the lights of a nearby ship. Evans decided to send the ship a courtesy message, letting them know that the *Californian* was stopped and surrounded by ice. At the time, Jack Phillips, the young radio operator on the *Titanic,* was busily trying to relay a backlog of personal messages from his passengers to a wireless radio tower in Newfoundland. Because the *Titanic* and the *Californian* were in such close proximity, Cyril Evans's radio message blasted loudly in Phillips's headphones. Annoyed, Phillips shot back, "Shut up! Shut up! I'm working Cape Race!"

Considering his duty done, Evans went to his cabin and fell asleep. All through the peculiar events of the late night and early morning, he slept undisturbed and unaware.

Considering his duty done, Evans went to his cabin and fell asleep. All through the peculiar events of the late night and early morning, he slept undisturbed and unaware. In fact, he did not get up the next morning until the chief officer awakened him to receive messages from two vessels that were radioing about the fate of the *Titanic*.

It was a moment that could have made Cyril Evans a hero. It could have been his "rendezvous with destiny." But he was asleep. Some historians have suggested that, even from only eight or nine miles away, the *Californian* could not have reached the scene in time to pluck people from the frigid North Atlantic waters before they drowned or died of hypothermia, but we'll never know for sure. Had Evans been awake, he at least would have received the *Titanic's* distress signals, and Captain Lord would have had the opportunity to attempt a rescue. Instead, the *Californian* has gone down in history as the ship that was closest to the scene and didn't help.

History is often made in the most ordinary moments, when people remain faithful to the task at hand. Frank Wills, the security guard, did his routine job so well that he stumbled onto a discovery that rocked our nation. For Cyril Evans, making a historic difference could have been as simple as staying awake and on the job.

5 all the small things

The biggest hurdle we face with creating small change is our inability to believe that small changes can make a big difference. We want big results, but we question whether small change will take us there. We can imagine how the world would change if we saw our dreams come to life, but we can't imagine that those world-changing dreams could start in such a small way.

Imagine this. It's a Thursday

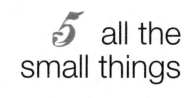

in December. It's already dark outside, and a woman named Rosa is just getting off work from her dead-end job hemming pants. Tired after a long day, she's grateful to find a seat on the bus. It's a route and a routine she's followed more times than she can remember. But today, something is going to be different.

On December 1, 1955, Rosa Parks boarded a bus for home and took an aisle seat next to some other African Americans in the front row of the "colored" section. A few stops later, as the bus filled up, some white passengers boarded and were unable to find seats. As was customary in Montgomery, Alabama, in those days, the bus driver simply shifted the boundary of the white section and expected the passengers seated there to move toward the back of the bus. In compliance with the driver's demand, three black passengers gave up their seats, but Rosa Parks simply moved over to the window seat and sat back down. When she refused to move, the bus driver called the police and had her arrested for violating a city ordinance.

On that first day of December, Mrs. Parks made a small change that affected the course of American history. But that wasn't what she set out to do. She did not speak with an eloquence that would command attention or earn her recognition. When she took her seat on the bus, she wasn't trying to stir up controversy. She did not know that thousands of other people would back her up and support her, or that the African American community in Montgomery would subsequently organize a bus boycott as a result of her arrest. She had no idea she was making history. All she knew was that she was not going to give up her seat.

She had no idea she was making history. All she knew was that she was not going to give up her seat.

Rosa Parks may have dreamed of changing the world. Certainly, she wanted to see a world without segregation. Her dream was no different from that of most African Americans at that time. But Rosa Parks acted on that dream. She saw a glimpse of her world-changing dream in a small change—in moving to the window seat to allow a white person to sit down. That one small change gave birth to a much bigger change, but it might not have happened if she had tried to shoot the moon and go for the big change all at once. It was her small, simple change that made the difference.

WORKING FOR THE WEEKEND

What would you have done in Rosa Parks's place? It was just another Thursday, another bus ride home. I suspect that for most of us, Friday would've been on our minds. The weekend was right around the corner. One more day between work and play. For many people, it seems, nothing exciting happens during the week. They're doing work that others require. It's not their passion or their purpose. But on the weekend . . . weekends are their opportunity to do something they love, to pursue what they really want to do.

Despising small things leads to ignoring them, avoiding them, and eventually trying to escape them altogether.

Why do we wait for the weekend? Is it because we despise the week? And do we aim for the grand because we despise the ordinary? Despising small things leads to ignoring them, avoiding them, and eventually trying to escape them altogether. But if we're waiting for the weekend to do the things we really care about, we're no longer living to work, we're merely working to live. And in the meantime . . . well, we miss the meantime. We miss the opportunities that present themselves during the week, during the majority of our waking lives. Before we know it, our whole lives can become "the week" while we're waiting for our shot at greatness.

For many followers of Jesus, it seems that heaven can become a kind of weekend and life on earth is that necessary evil, the longest week. We end up dreaming about "flying away" and looking for the Friday afternoon when we can leave it all behind. But having this weekend mentality is an obstacle to making the kind of lasting change our world needs. It causes us to forget about the little things we've been given to do right here.

FAITHFUL WITH LITTLE

When we left the story of Nehemiah, he was weeping. He had just heard of the dismal conditions in his homeland and of his beloved capital, Jerusalem. The Jews of Judah had been in exile for more than seventy years as punishment for their repeated disobedience and disregard for God. But they knew the promise that they would one day return home.

Nehemiah had grown up in Persia, and now served in the palace in Susa. Although it was all he had known, it was not home to him. Hope had begun to rise when he heard that some Jews had already begun to return to Jerusalem. Could it be that God would restore the greatness of his people in Nehemiah's generation, returning them to their land and fulfilling their promised destiny? The news of Jerusalem's devastation—the walls that had once surrounded the city like a giant fortress now broken and burned, and the shame that covered those who lived there—sucked the hope from his heart and the oxygen from his lungs. The news was no longer secondhand folklore; he had heard the disastrous truth from his own brother's lips.

Shock and grief overwhelmed him physically. For days, Nehemiah could not eat but filled every moment with prayer to the God of his people. Nehemiah was so overcome with sorrow that he repented of all of his sins, and those of his family. He reiterated God's vow to scatter his people if they disobeyed, fully acknowledging the reason for their punishment. He also reminded God that if the people returned and obeyed, God had promised to return them to their homeland, even if they were exiled to the farthest reaches of the earth. Nehemiah wanted this to be the turning point. He wanted his life to be a spiritual hinge for his entire nation. He desperately wanted his life to affect the situation.

Sound familiar? Like Nehemiah, we are moved beyond emotion when we see the condition of our brothers and sisters. We feel great hope and deep pride in being the unstoppable, called-out ones, yet we're painfully aware of the sin in our own lives and the faults in so many of our institutions. Nevertheless, like Nehemiah, we must speak of our own—the church—as "us," not "them."

We have sinned, and we are the people of God. We are the ones God promised to use to spread his salvation to the ends of the earth. If we return to him, he will bring us back to a place of influence and purpose from which all peoples will be blessed. The problem for us, as it was for Nehemiah, is figuring out how we should help.

Nehemiah was a cupbearer to the Persian king, Artaxerxes. That might sound like a glamorous job—until you find out what it entailed. Nehemiah's responsibility was to taste the king's wine before the king did, to make sure it wasn't poisoned. So, every day when he showed up for work, he was literally one sip away from death.

Think about that for a second. Maybe you're in a job that isn't all you hoped for or isn't your life's dream, but would you like to trade places with Nehemiah?

We've all had jobs that we hated, but how many have had a job where success or failure was literally a life or death proposition? For a Starbucks barista, a bad day means spilled coffee, an irritated manager, or some grouchy customers. For a grocery store clerk, a bad day means haggling over prices and pennies. For a professional dog walker, a bad day means running out of those plastic bags for . . . well, you know. But for Nehemiah, a bad day meant he was dead. It's possible the only reason he got the job in the first place was that his predecessor had vacated the position, if you know what I mean.

> *No amount of money could compel a man to risk his life and health every day, but personal convictions of a deeper sort could make a man trustworthy in the face of such danger.*

Cupbearers were completely dispensable, yet they had to be profoundly trustworthy. That is a testimony to Nehemiah's character. The job added little meaning to his life and required very little skill or intelligence. But it demanded noble qualities of character with few rewards. A cupbearer's performance had to be driven by motives deeper than compensation, a great retirement package, or personal well-being. No amount of money could compel a man to risk his life and health every day, but personal convictions of a deeper sort could make a man trustworthy in the face of such danger. Nehemiah had what it takes.

His thankless job held little potential for greatness. It was, by any standard, a small job, a job without dignity. Yet, Nehemiah persevered and served the king well. He proved himself faithful and trustworthy. In fact, until the report came from Jerusalem, the king had never seen Nehemiah have a bad day.

As anyone knows who has lived with grief, life moves forward without compassion. Nehemiah soon found himself back in the palace of the king, exhausted from his mourning, and spent from imploring God to honor his promise to restore Jerusalem.

His grief was not something he could hide. He recalled, "Early the following spring . . . I was serving the king his wine. I had never before appeared sad in his presence. So the king asked me, 'Why are you looking so sad? You don't look sick to me. You must be deeply troubled.'"[2]

Now, I have a great job—and maybe you do too—but I can't say that I've always shown up for work in the best frame of mind. And when I'm having a bad day, the people around me know it. But that's not the way it was with Nehemiah. In all the time he served the king, putting his life on the line every day, he had maintained a cheerful, good-natured spirit. That's what made it so remarkable the one day when he appeared sad.

FAITHFULNESS AND FAVOR

Startled that the king was actually talking to him, and even more amazed by the king's question, Nehemiah was instantly terrified. Gathering his composure, he responded, "Long live the king! How can I not be sad? For the city where my ancestors are buried is in ruins, and the gates have been destroyed by fire." Nehemiah must have thought he was dreaming when he heard the king ask, "Well, how can I help you?"[3]

Nehemiah's courage began to grow as he recognized the king's favor. "If it please the king, and if you are pleased with me, your servant, send me to Judah to rebuild the city where my ancestors are buried." The next verse says the king had the queen sitting beside him, and as I imagine it he suddenly became aware of her and momentarily snapped out of his benevolent mood. He pressed Nehemiah for more details: "How long will you be gone? When will you return?"[4]

Nehemiah and the king then spent the next few minutes working out an agreeable timetable. Nehemiah grew bold enough to ask the king for letters to the governors of the surrounding provinces that would grant him safe passage. He also asked for a letter to the manager of the king's forests so that he could get the timber he needed to rebuild the Temple gates, the city walls, and a home for himself. The king granted everything he asked for.

Nehemiah won the king's favor for his great request because he had always been faithful in small tasks.

Here is the point: Nehemiah won the king's favor for his great request because he had always been faithful in small tasks. It's precisely because of his record of excellent, joyful service that his day of sorrow was noticed. Because Nehemiah had always served the king well, the king was ready and willing to help Nehemiah in unprecedented ways. Nehemiah demonstrated excellence in the way that American statesman John W. Gardner once described as "doing ordinary things extraordinarily well."[5]

There's a lesson to be learned there for all of us. By being faithful in the small things of life, Nehemiah earned the favor of the king, which opened the door to greater things to come. Like Jesus said, "If you are faithful in little things, you will be faithful in large ones. But if you are dishonest in little things, you won't be honest with greater responsibilities."[6] Nehemiah learned faithfulness in small tasks, and it opened the door to some pretty big opportunities.

GRASS ROOTS WORSHIP

Every Friday night, I get to lead college-age students in reckless, passionate worship. On Sunday mornings, I stand alongside a great team of friends to lead our whole church family in worship. During the week, I get to work with young people who are training to be worship leaders for churches. And to top it off, I get to travel with Desperation Band to conferences and churches around the country, leading worship and telling the story of what God is doing in our midst. But it's possible that none of this would have unfolded if not for a young high school girl who took a small step.

When I was thirteen or fourteen, the junior high group at my church in Malaysia needed someone to lead worship. One of the youth leaders—a high school girl who was helping out with the junior high group—asked me if I would be willing to do it. My immediate response was, "No, I don't think that's my calling." The truth is, I was simply too scared. Fortunately, the youth leader was persistent and asked me to try it just once. So, with some hesitation, I agreed.

For me, as a teenager who loved God and music, that

one chance to lead worship was the biggest deal in my world. For a month before my scheduled day of leading worship, I fell asleep every night going through song lists in my head. (I know, I'm weird.) Looking back, that opportunity seems like such a small event, on such a small scale, but its implications for my life were huge.

Leading worship quickly became a regular part of my junior high and high school years, and by the time I went to college, I was ready to dedicate my life to leading worship and teaching—and all because a high school girl did her ordinary task of coordinating junior high worship extraordinarily well. She didn't just ask me and let me decline. She was faithful to take the second small step of encouraging me to at least give it a shot. Her simple word of encouragement—a small flap of a butterfly's wings—had an impact that altered the course of my life.

PAY IT FORWARD

After college, I joined the staff of the university as a worship leader. After a year of that, I really wanted to plug in at a local church and serve. My roommate's brother, Ross, was (and still is) the worship pastor at a church in Colorado that I really admired, New Life Church in Colorado Springs. I had visited on a few occasions and felt a real connection and calling.

When Ross offered me a one-year apprenticeship, I decided to accept it, even though I had received offers to be the main worship pastor at some other churches. I couldn't shake the sense that New Life was where I was supposed to be. But when I got there, it was hard not to feel as if I had taken a step backward. I went from leading worship for thousands of college students to making photocopies of music for the choir and setting up for choir rehearsals.

I went from leading worship for thousands of college students to making photocopies of music for the choir and setting up for choir rehearsals.

I tried to do it well. I did it as well as I could. But, I'll be honest. On the inside, I was thinking, *Four months ago I was leading worship with five thousand students. Now I'm not leading anywhere. I play the piano on Sunday mornings.*

The biggest opportunity I had to lead worship was for our newly begun college ministry, called theMILL, which had about thirty or forty people at the time. From five thousand to forty, that's a big difference, and it was challenging. Yet, I realized it was my turn to be faithful in small things. Just as that youth leader had been faithful to encourage me to lead worship when I was fourteen, I now had to be faithful with the small, simple tasks given to me. Instead of paying her back, I had to pay it forward—just like in the movie—by being faithful now. I began to put a lot of time and effort into it. I began to get excited about it, and jumped in as much as I could.

The faithfulness of those before us has opened the

doors for us to be where we are. Should we squander the opportunities? Should we not follow in their footsteps and be faithful with what we have been given to do?

I meet people from time to time who find a round-about way of asking me how they can get a job like mine. I think of the words of an old preacher to a bunch of young upstart ministers: "You want to do what I do, but you don't want to do what I did." The people who come up to me didn't see what the job looked like six years ago. The truth is, God put me in this place and gave me the strength to keep going, and then he blessed it. Because of the faithfulness of Aaron Stern, theMILL's pastor, and a host of volunteers, God has continued to add people to our gatherings. Today, more than a thou-sand college-age young people come to theMILL every Friday night. If any of us who were there at the start would have bailed when the going got tough and it looked like the group would never grow, we would have missed out on so much that we've learned through the process.

D. L. Moody said, "There are many of us that are willing to do great things for the Lord, but few of us are willing to do little things."[7] If we don't prove ourselves faithful in all the small things, God will never entrust to us the bigger investments. If we fail to meet God in the little things, we run the risk of never seeing God work at all.

6 big dreams

Every college student is an idealist, but my years on campus were full of something beyond idealism. It was more like idealism on steroids. That's because I went to a wonderful but strange Christian university. The second question most people asked (right after "What's your name?") was "What's God calling you to do?" Even more amazing was that everyone seemed to have an answer, like they expected to be asked! After a few weeks of being awkwardly involved in these strange getting-to-know-you rituals, I wondered if people were starting to drum up answers to the question so as not be left out.

"Me? Oh, um, God is calling me to start a hospital in Uganda . . . that will have its own record label . . . um . . . where the patients will write songs . . . and . . . um . . . the profits will fund cancer research."

"Wow!" *(Long, breathless pause)*

"Yes." *(Smug look of satisfaction, knowing that you've made the desired impression)*

It seemed like the more bizarre your dream or vision, the greater the sense that it was divinely inspired. All this made discussions about ambitions and career goals really strange. If at a normal college you might talk about your plans to become a millionaire before you turned thirty, at my college, you would talk about how God was going to make you a millionaire before you turned thirty—it was his will and your destiny. Nobody could tell us that we were simply textbook examples of youthful optimism, bravado, and naivete; in our minds, we were just full of faith. I remember listening to countless sermons about how we could do this or that great thing, if only we would believe. (You know, the old "If you can believe it, you can achieve it" speech.)

And I believed. As did many of my peers. We sat around the cafeteria, dreaming out loud about the things that would make us famous. Over fried chicken and yet another bowl of country gravy–covered mash, we talked about the foundations we'd start, the countries we would entirely convert to Christianity, and our plans for eradicating AIDS from the continent of Africa.

Nobody could tell us that we were simply textbook examples of youthful optimism, bravado, and naivete; in our minds, we were just full of faith.

Today, almost ten years later, I am proud of the way many of my friends are serving God, faithfully working at the things he has placed in their lives. The dreams that seemed so far away are gradually coming to pass. But some of my dining hall companions with big dreams don't have jobs that even remotely resemble what they so passionately described over chicken and potatoes. Some have become so discouraged that they've given up on their dreams completely, and even abandoned their faith. Optimism turned to cynicism in less than a decade. What went wrong?

DOWN BUT NOT OUT

It seems so natural for youthful dreams to be struck a deadly blow by the realities of life. In fact, we've almost come to expect it. The storyline seems inevitable: Start with dreams, have them dashed in dramatic fashion, and then make your peace with a cynical mediocrity.

Yet, we all still have yearnings, deeply held desires to be and to do something extraordinary. Our dreams come from the belief that things can be different, that change for the better can occur, and that the world will not always be the way it is now. Our dreams ignite the

flame of hope inside us. But we know that hope is a diz-
zying elixir. We understand that "hope, as a rule, makes
many a fool." Nobody wants to play the fool.

It seems that many people today take one of two
approaches when it comes to their dreams: Either dream
big and fall short, or don't dream at all. These days, the
latter path seems more popular. Having been a witness
to a few decades of church kids falling short of their
youth group dreams, I've seen how many young people
today seem to prefer slipping into the role of critical
observer, opting out of the mainstream, declining to
try—or even to aim. It's so much easier, instead, to grab
their laptops and retreat to the corner of the neighbor-
hood coffeehouse, staring out the window writing blogs
about how everybody else is living. This often cynical
perspective is seen as somehow more *authentic* or honest.

> *The sort of faith we develop
> by opting out, and choosing
> instead to observe and critique,
> is a faith that does not give
> birth to dreams. . . . Faith
> must be tested in order to be
> made stronger.*

The problem is that the sort of faith we develop by
opting out, and choosing instead to observe and cri-
tique, is a faith that does not give birth to dreams. It

is a faith so riddled by fear of a letdown that dreaming itself is virtually banished. Faith must be tested in order to be made stronger. When the dreams our faith gave rise to don't come true, we must turn to God, the object of our faith, not away from him. As the apostle Paul writes, "We are pressed on every side by troubles, but we are not crushed. We are perplexed, but not driven to despair. We are hunted down, but never abandoned by God. We get knocked down, but we are not destroyed."[1]

What so often happens, though, is that shattered dreams lead to a shaken faith. We begin to question whether we understand God's plans at all—or God himself, for that matter. We also call into question the Christian environment that gave rise to our dreams. We're disenchanted by anything that feels too much like "church"—the place where our dreams were first stirred and we were encouraged to believe that God could use us to change the world—or we're embarrassed by it, like a high school kid at the mall with his mom.

But high school kids are supposed to grow out of that stage. We've got to find a way to get over ourselves, as large of an obstacle as we are. After all, cynicism is the first sign of self-importance. The world is bigger than our identity crises. Our faith is older than its critics. The sooner we realize that, the sooner we'll leave our adolescent faith for a mature faith better suited to our adult lives.

The world is not perfect. All is not as the Designer intended. But rather than resigning ourselves to a wishful mediocrity, hoping our lives will somehow matter, or assuming the role of cynical commentator, can we not engage with our culture and take the necessary steps to put our dreams into action? The world has not lost its need for dreamers. It just needs dreamers who will learn from history and develop workable, biblical strategies; dreamers with a childlike innocence and a mature faith.

Maybe my friends from the dining hall were wrong from the start. Maybe they dreamed of doing what no single human being could possibly do. No individual, no matter how gifted or determined, can accomplish what some of my peers set out to achieve. They were trying to change the world, a goal that young Christians are often encouraged to pursue. But we cannot change the world by making it our goal. It would be a waste of our lives to make changing the world our aim. Trying to change the world is the surest way to guarantee that we won't. In aiming for the world, we often miss the opportunities right in front of us. We can become so fixated on the fantastic that we fail to do anything that matters at all in the here and now.

World-changers choose to focus on change in their present circumstances by translating their big dreams into daily action.

Like Rosa Parks, people who change the world typically don't have that as their goal. Far-reaching change is a by-product of more immediate choices and values.

World-changers choose to focus on change in their present circumstances by translating their big dreams into
daily action. It doesn't mean they're not still dreaming
big; it just means they're taking action on achievable
objectives at the local level. They know that large-scale
change starts with individual action.

Creating lasting change and achieving big goals
are consequences of a series of smaller actions. We've
already established that. But beyond that, widespread
change is the eventual consequence of actions done *in
a particular place*. That is the second secret of creating
lasting change: Change is local.

Dreaming of big changes and broad influence isn't
wrong, but it can distract us from doing the day-to-day
work that actually brings massive, lasting change. As
great as big dreams are, they can actually prevent us
from ever getting started. Sometimes, the small steps,
the local actions, feel so far from where we want to end
up that we never take the first steps or work within
our immediate context. We need to practice the faith of
Nehemiah—being diligent in our daily cupbearing while
at the same time pursuing our dreams. God knows the
whole story from beginning to end, and he is at work to
bring his purposes to completion.

BE UNORIGINAL

We may have a grand vision of what God has called us
to do, but the next step is always to ask him, "Lord,
what do I do *right here?*" Don't wait for the "somewhere
out there." Don't wait for a different platform or a different opportunity. What are the platforms and opportunities within your sphere of influence right now? Start

there. Everyone has a sphere of influence right where they are.

> *Many young dreamers have a tendency to want to start something new, rather than join a good work already in progress.*

I've noticed that so many young dreamers have a tendency to want to start something new, rather than join a good work already in progress. Some of this, I suspect, comes from disappointment with the status quo. But just as much, I think, comes from pride—they want to start something they can put their mark on, something dramatic that hasn't been done before. But the point isn't to do something dramatic or original. The point is God and his kingdom! We've got to let God into the ordinary moments and the unspectacular locations of our lives to see what *he* wants to do there. God is the one who is building his kingdom. We can't do it ourselves, because we don't know which moments, which actions, which decisions are going to contribute to the furthering of God's story.

Instead of asking, "What can I start?" we should be asking, "Where can I serve?" In pursuing our dreams and passions by serving, we gain momentum and direction. Then, if there's truly nothing out there that fits a specific need, or maybe in the course of serving we find something else that's more important, then we can move on to ask, "What can I start?" But "where can I serve?" should always come first.

What we're really after is lasting change. The kind of change worth recording is the kind that endures long after we're gone. Any change that affects a person, an organization, or a country on a deep level, in a far-reaching way, with long-lasting effects starts with local action. Change doesn't happen out there, up there, or in the future. Lasting change is the result of acting here and now. It doesn't happen on a worldwide scale but in local, within-your-reach places.

DEFINING DESPERATION

One of the ways the principle of local change plays out in my world is the way in which Desperation Band has remained true to its identity as a local church worship band. In recent years, the band has experienced a measure of what some would call success. With significant album sales and widely popular original songs such as "I Am Free," "Rescue," and "Amazed," we have had some great opportunities open up to us. But Desperation Band is nothing more than the worship of the student ministries of our church. The "band" as an entity only began when we got together some of the people leading worship for our high school and college ministries at our church to lead for our first summer student ministry conference in 2002. The conference was titled "Desperation," and the band was named accordingly.

When the original songs that came from our team were recorded at our Desperation conferences and other gatherings of our student ministries, Integrity Music decided to release our albums on their record label. With the increased exposure and influence came the opportunity to travel and play at other churches and conferences.

That was also a moment of decision. Who were we going to be? A traveling worship artist band that loosely plugs in to our local church, or a local church worship band that occasionally travels? The answer was easy. As my fellow songwriter and worship leader Jon Egan says, "We can't affect hundreds of churches; but we can affect one."

We are called to serve our local church. That's priority number one. What it means for us is that we never miss more than one youth service, college service, or Sunday morning service a month. And if for some reason we need to, it requires our pastor's approval. On every other Wednesday night, Friday night, and Sunday, you can find us serving our local church—onstage or off.

GO HOME

The Gospel writer Mark tells the story of Jesus delivering a madman from demons. A mob of evil spirits had plagued this man, making him wander about in graveyards, screaming and slashing himself with sharp rocks. When Jesus drove out the demons and sent them into a herd of swine, the madman became almost unrecognizably different. Now he was "wearing decent clothes and making sense."[2] Deeply moved by the miraculous power that had radically freed and transformed him, the man begged Jesus to let him go with him.

Perhaps the man would have followed Jesus to the

edge of the sea as he was preparing to leave by boat. I imagine him being out of breath, and rambling a bit as he tries to convince Jesus to take him along.

I hear him say: "Jesus! You are something special! I am a totally different person! What you've done in me . . . *wow!* How can I repay you? Jesus, let me go with you. Let me travel with you to the other towns. I can tell the people my story. I'll be your opening act. After they hear my testimony, they'll be primed for your teaching and for more miracles. Jesus! We can't keep this a secret! Everyone needs to know who you are."

We don't have to guess at how Jesus responded. Mark tells us. I'm sure Jesus smiled warmly at the man as he said, "Go home to your own people. Tell them your story—what the Master did, how he had mercy on you."[3]

We have big dreams because we've had an encounter with a colossal God.

We have big dreams because we've had an encounter with a colossal God. He's stepped in and changed us deeply and miraculously. The difference is undeniable. Our natural response is, "God, let's take this show on the road! Let's tell everyone." Jesus doesn't rebuke the former madman for wanting to tell everyone; neither does he chasten us for wanting to change the world. Those are good, God-given impulses. He responds, instead, by telling the man—and us—*how* to change the world by not trying to change the world.

Imagine Jesus looking into your eyes with his warm smile. He sees your big dreams. He knows your desire to create massive change because of the massive change you've experienced. But he wants you to know that your opportunities to change the world are not waiting for you in the future, they're waiting for you to start right now. He wants you to look around you, to find something you could be a part of. No, it may not be glamorous, glorious, or brimming with the destiny you've been dreaming of. But your opportunity is something somewhere that needs to change; you can see it, and you can affect it. That's where lasting change starts—right there, in the small spaces and the in-betweens of our lives. So he gently says to you, as he says to me, "Go home. Tell your people the story of what God has done in you."

7 yourspace

On October 31, 1517, an ordinary man did a particular thing in a specific place that had the most extraordinary and far-reaching consequences. Martin Luther, a thirty-five-year-old preacher and professor in Wittenberg, Saxony (present-day Germany), summarized three of his sermons in the form of ninety-five concise statements and nailed them to the door of the parish church, "which served as the 'blackboard' of the university, on which all notices of disputations and high academic functions were displayed."[1] Luther's act "was not an open declaration of war, but simply an academic challenge to a disputation."[2]

"The Disputation on the Power and the Efficacy of Indulgences," or, as we now know them, the Ninety-five Theses, created more than a small stir. Greatly aided by the newly invented printing press, copies of Luther's treatise were made and distributed all over Saxony. Before long, the pope issued an edict (called a papal bull), declaring Luther a heretic. He was ordered to appear before Emperor Charles V to recant his writings.

Luther refused to recant, and was rescued and hidden by his patron Frederick the Wise, elector of Saxony. Frederick was fond of Luther and intrigued by his teachings. His choice to defend Luther, even in defiance of the pope, led to a breach with the Roman Catholic Church and paved the way for the spread of what became known as Protestantism.

The newfound freedom from the papacy in the Protestant countries of Northern Europe resulted in a proliferation of new ideas and led to the rapid intellectual advancement of European culture in the seventeenth and eighteenth centuries. This shift eventually gave rise to the era that we now call the Age of Reason.

Did Luther intend to accomplish all that? Not likely.

Earlier in 1517, a Dominican monk named Johann Tetzel had been commissioned by the pope to sell indulgences—certificates that purported to grant partial or full remission of time in purgatory for the buyer or his or her loved ones. The indulgences were issued in an effort to raise funds for the building of St. Peter's

Basilica in Rome to protect the relics of St. Paul and St. Peter.

Tetzel was a slick salesman. He might even be considered the father of modern marketing, with his coinage of the catchy slogan, "As soon as the coin in the coffer rings, a soul from purgatory springs."

Armed with his indulgences for sale, Tetzel was assigned the territory of Saxony. His often theatrical presentation moved many to buy these indulgences, including many in Martin Luther's parish. Luther, already enraged by the notion of the power of relics, was shocked and saddened that many of his own parishioners were caught up in this latest superstition. Shortly after Tetzel's visit, Luther wrote and posted his Ninety-five Theses.

He was fighting for individuals, not for some grand cause.

Was nailing his protest to the door of his own small and somewhat obscure church the best way to disseminate his message? No, it seems he would have done better to have sent a letter to the pope, or perhaps to protest outside the Vatican. But Luther didn't care about that. Not to begin with. He was trying to save his own people from their ignorance. No doubt he knew their names, their stories, their aspirations, and their trepidations. He was fighting for individuals, not for some grand cause. Still, by acting to defend and rescue his own congregants,

Martin Luther changed the world. He stirred the air with his own two wings and set in motion changes that would upend some of the foundations of the Roman Catholic Church. The change started locally, it happened in small increments, and it happened over a long period of time.

The Reformation that Luther sparked is a classic example of how change works. He began by taking a small step to act within his local environment. He tacked his message to a door. In our day and age, we may not pay much attention to the flyers we see posted on coffee shop or grocery store bulletin boards, or on roadside telephone poles. But in Luther's day, that's how information was disseminated. He simply nailed his thoughts on the door of the local church, the center of community activity.

What Luther could not have anticipated was that his Ninety-five Theses would soon gain a broader audience through the use of a fairly recent innovation known as the printing press. Invented in 1447 by Johannes Gutenberg, the printing press expanded the range of influence that one individual could have, by making it possible to duplicate and distribute information much more widely than hand-copying would allow.

As Luther's Ninety-five Theses were published throughout Saxony and beyond, his ideas gained an audience and developed the sort of momentum necessary to take root in the public mind. For Luther, the printing press expanded the definition of *local* far beyond his own little town of Wittenberg. In our day, with technological advances that Luther could not have even dreamed of, creating lasting change involves using the tools in our hands to expand our own definition of *local*.

EXPANDING YOUR "LOCAL"

The global age, ushered in by the pervasive expansion of the Internet, is now in full bloom. We have become instantly accessible via cell phones, BlackBerries, and wireless Internet access. We can disseminate our every thought through blogs, vlogs, and podcasts. We can maintain long-distance friendships and continue building international relationships at high speed. The belief that we're limited by where we are is a relic of the past.

As businesses have learned to capitalize on the advances in communications technology—such as the fiber-optic cables that now tie the world together—the capacity to do things across international borders is virtually limitless. New software has been created that makes it possible for ordinary, non-technical people to record their own music, create their own Web sites, and start their own online businesses. Moreover, companies, even young start-ups, can employ people and sell to people they have never met and never will. The entrance of thousands of Indians and Chinese to the global work-force—not as sweatshop workers, but as customer support personnel and highly skilled technical workers—has changed how work is done. More to the point, it has changed *where* work is done.

I work for an organization that has a virtual private network (VPN). Technically, it means I can work from anywhere that has Internet access. Functionally, it means I'm always working. I could be sitting in the airport in Kuala Lumpur, Malaysia, and access files, e-mails, and whatever else I need on our company's shared network in Colorado Springs. I can even add data and resources to the network so that my colleagues—wherever in the world they might be—can access the information. I have the ability to affect situations, discussions, and decisions beyond my precise geographic location.

> *I have the ability to affect situations, discussions, and decisions beyond my precise geographic location.*

Another example of capitalizing on the opportunities afforded us, in what Thomas Friedman calls the "flat world," is the virtual community known as MySpace, which had more than 42 million members only two years after its initial launch. MySpace members can create their own pages, add "friends," post songs or blogs or pictures, and send and receive e-mails, comments, or instant messages with other MySpace users.

MySpace also has a special section for bands and singer/songwriters. Many independent bands have used the site to launch themselves and increase their exposure. Bands can post song files to be downloaded or accessed as streaming audio. "Friends" can post the songs on their own pages so their network of friends (who may otherwise never hear of the band) can "discover" the latest sound and in turn request to be added to the band's list of "friends."

It used to be (and not that long ago) that a band had to rely on its record label to get the news out—or I suppose they could put up flyers around town. But now, through MySpace and other online locations, a band can virtually "put up flyers" all over the world—*and* they can make their music instantly available to millions of people who otherwise would most likely never hear of them.

And the benefits don't end there. Not only can a band keep a very detailed and easily accessible mailing list of its fan base (complete with pictures), but the fans—or *friends,* as MySpace calls them—can also see who the band's other friends are, read their comments, and interact with them.

Consider the story of Dane Cook, a stand-up comedian. Until 2001, Cook was barely known outside his loyal, word-of-mouth following. Though he had been doing stand-up as a full-time career since 1993, he had not achieved anything that could be called a breakthrough.

Then, in 2001, the Comedy Channel aired a half-hour special featuring Cook. His fan base and popularity soon achieved critical mass, thanks in large part to his Web site and his page on MySpace. By 2005, Cook had amassed well over 650,000 "friends" on MySpace, all of whom feel like they know him—at least, that's the impression you get when you read their comments.

By late 2005, Dane was invited to be a guest host on *Saturday Night Live,* hallowed ground for some of the world's best-loved comedians. He has since performed at a sold-out Madison Square Garden, and his comic CD was listed on *Billboard* magazine's top five for 2005. (To put that achievement in context, a comedy CD had not cracked *Billboard*'s top five since Steve Martin's *Wild and Crazy Guy* in 1978.) Is it purely coincidental that Dane Cook's accelerated success parallels the rise of MySpace?

Inspired by Cook, I've created my own MySpace page, though not for comedy. To be honest, it took me a while to jump on the bandwagon. My first impression was that the site was merely for people who were looking for a souped-up version of online dating, or for bands that didn't have a record label. After much persuasion and careful investigation, I realized that I could use MySpace for . . . whatever I want! Once I joined, I was shocked to discover how many friends I had who were already making full use of the site—not to mention all the major bands and artists who were building and maintaining their massive fan bases.

Now I'm a MySpace junkie—constantly checking my page, adding friends, and posting comments. It's gotten a little out of hand. This past Thanksgiving, while visiting my in-laws at their farm in Iowa, I was able to keep track of all my MySpace friends, while watching a herd of cattle grazing outside.

Earlier in the day, I had helped my father-in-law and the local veterinarian vaccinate more than sixty heifers and bulls. Later that evening, as we sat by the fire, my father-in-law showed me an article in the town paper about a guy in rural Minnesota who was about to conduct an online cattle auction. This ain't your grandpa's farm.

Because this cattle rancher has learned how to expand his definition of *local* by making use of existing technology, my father-in-law, and countless others, could save time and hundreds of dollars in travel expenses by participating in the online auction. We're not talking about a multinational conglomerate; this is a farmer from rural Minnesota. Acting locally sure has changed.

ANYTHING WITHIN YOUR REACH

If change starts locally, and *local* can now be defined as "anything within your reach," how do we work within a global community with technology that affords us virtually unlimited reach? I think the best answer is to focus on the abilities and resources that we can control.

Stephen Covey, in his classic self-management book *The 7 Habits of Highly Effective People,* explains the difference between a person's "circle of concern" and his or her "circle of influence." Our *circle of concern* is everything that consumes our thoughts and emotions, the causes we are passionate about—regardless of whether we have any control over them. Our *circle of influence,* on the other hand, is everything we can actually shape or affect.

It's a waste of time to expend energy on things that are not within our circle of influence—even if they're within our reach. It only leads to a sense of hopelessness and frustration, like a school kid trying to boycott exams. But sometimes there are things in our circle of concern—things we are passionate about—that we can bring into our circle of influence. That's where technology comes in.

If we can give advice to a friend in France from our computer in Cleveland, then France is local for us. If we can get on a plane in Pittsburgh and fly to an orphanage in Uruguay, that's local.

I have a friend who moved to Turkey with his wife to start a covert movement to evangelize remote villages. Another friend is an engineer in China, where he and his wife reach people that may have never met a preacher or a Christian that isn't a peasant. My job is in Colorado Springs, but I also travel across the country as a member of Desperation Band. Local for me is both places—where I live and where I go. As our concept of "local" has changed, the potential for our influence to affect a broader spectrum of the world has increased.

> *As our concept of "local" has changed, the potential for our influence to affect a broader spectrum of the world has increased.*

Of course, as our reach has expanded, so has everyone else's. Because of that, the number of influences we have to filter through has also increased. We might be receiving input—wanted and unwanted, good and bad—from ten times as many sources as we did ten years ago. The key for us is to focus our local efforts on a specific locale. Instead of spreading our influence in all directions, we should focus on a few specific locations. It's the difference between the light from a glowing lightbulb and the beam of a laser.

STAYING FOCUSED

There's a great bumper sticker out there that sums it all up: *Think Globally. Act Locally.* Dream big, but act within your reach.

It's important to keep the big picture—God's storyline—always in view, because it can guide our decisions when the way is uncertain, and inspire our

passion when we face adversity. When the changes we
make seem small and insignificant, or frustratingly narrow and local, the big picture can encourage us to stay
the course and keep at it. Staying the course can be difficult when our vision is limited to our own experience
and circumstances, and change seems to take much longer than we think it should.

> *When the changes we make
> seem small and insignificant,
> or frustratingly narrow and
> local, the big picture can
> encourage us to stay the course
> and keep at it.*

But let's not forget that God works in very ordinary
ways, and we don't know which ordinary moment is
going to make the difference in someone's life. That
doesn't mean spreading ourselves thin to do as many
small things as we can manage. It means doing one
thing well, and sticking with it. More on that later.

World-changers don't necessarily *try* to be world-
changers. It's too broad an aim. Creating change is a
consequence of a particular action in a specific place
and time. Changing the world doesn't happen by trying
to affect the whole world and creating big change all
at once. Changing the world starts with a single, small
action. And that action must happen here and now,
right where we are.

8 farewell to fireworks

Change happens at
lightning speed these days. We can
get so many things immediately that we
begin to expect instant results on everything. Lose fifty pounds—overnight!
Have abs or buns of steel—in just thirty
minutes! Become a millionaire—by
reading this book! There is an ever-
expanding list of fads that are hot
today and history by the time you
read this. And not the good kind of

history, but just warmed-up, leftover, last-year's news. That's because most of the change that happens today, the change that happens at lightning speed, is change that doesn't last. Everything becomes obsolete—and it seems that many things are even designed that way. (Feeling dumb with your one-color, non-video iPod?)

At the Rock and Roll Hall of Fame in Cleveland, there's an exhibit devoted to keeping alive the memories of one-hit wonders—like Wild Cherry, remember them? The band came out of eastern Ohio, "dancin' and singin' and movin' to the groovin'." They were picked up by Epic Records and their first album went platinum in 1976 on the shoulders of one song, "Play That Funky Music," which hit number one on the charts. The band received two Grammy nominations and won an American Music Award and a Billboard music award for their efforts. After a stellar debut, their subsequent four albums over the next three years flopped. Today, the only thing anyone remembers about Wild Cherry is their one hit song, which still turns up on playlists at weddings, and proms, right before "YMCA" and right after "Electric Boogie." Otherwise, they're just a memory, a blip on the collective consciousness of popular culture, quickly displaced by the next flaming supernova. And for every one-hit wonder immortalized in Cleveland there are countless other bands whose music died without fanfare.

We are a part of the collective consciousness, watching our cultural icons go off like fireworks on the Fourth of July. We're wowed by their bursts of light, but then quickly diverted to the next flash, and the next, the next, and the next. Soon we're shell-shocked and numb.

We forget the individual fireworks, even though we may remember the general experience. And when the fireworks are gone, there's nothing left but smoke and silence.

FAST TRACK TO NOWHERE

So, what is it about getting things quickly? From coffee to car insurance, we think that everything we require or desire should be available right this minute. But think back just a few years . . .

> *What is it about getting things quickly? From coffee to car insurance, we think that everything we require or desire should be available right this minute.*

Imagine I told you that you could access virtually any library in the world, browse a catalog of books or clothes, or find directions to anywhere from anywhere with the stroke of a few keys. You wouldn't have believed me. What if I told you that you might have to wait a few minutes before the information you requested appeared on your computer screen? You would have been happy to wait.

"You mean I can type in a simple phrase and the computer will find 10 million sources of information about that subject? No way!"

Your jaw would have dropped in disbelief as you told me that we were living in the greatest information era in history. Yet even the marvelous World Wide Web has fallen prey to our unyielding lust for immediacy.

"Dial-up? Are you serious? There's no way I'm using dial-up!" That well-known series of beeps followed by a fuzz of noise is now a symbol of antiquity. It's not good enough to have access to an unimaginable ocean of information—we need to have *high-speed* access to it.

> *As response times have diminished, so has that fruit of the Spirit known as patience.*

As response times have diminished, so has that fruit of the Spirit known as *patience*.

I was sitting in the Colorado Springs airport recently, waiting to fly out to a meeting, and my flight was delayed by an hour. You can imagine my indignation.

"A whole hour? What? I've got to be there . . . now!" Never mind that it would have taken me twelve hours or more to drive to my meeting. I wanted to get on that plane and take off without delay.

Our hunger for the immediate clouds our perspective and often crowds out our ability to be thankful. It also impairs our judgment. I can't tell you how often I've made a quick purchase, only to realize later that if I had just waited a few months, I could have gotten a newer, better—and, yes, *faster*—gadget for half the price. This temporary lack of judgment has its most severe consequences when it affects the way we think about creating or experiencing change. Even though we suspect deep down that nothing fast can last, we are so easily enticed by promises of immediate change.

Believing that change happens in sudden bursts makes perseverance seem pointless. Staying put and staying focused seem unnecessary if we believe that whatever change should have happened would have happened by now. If change doesn't happen in the brief span of time that we expect, then it only makes sense, it seems, to move on. Or maybe we don't move on; maybe we simply stop trying. We find ourselves disillusioned and without hope for making an impact. We give up and quit trying, quit persevering, quit expecting anything. We quit believing that real, lasting change can happen.

> *Believing that change happens in sudden bursts makes perseverance seem pointless. Staying put and staying focused seem unnecessary.*

If there's one place where that kind of thinking is clearly displayed, it's in vocational ministry. I've been an associate worship pastor at a church in Colorado for about seven years now. Many of the people I work with have been at the church a lot longer than I have. The main worship pastor has been there for fifteen years.

I never realized what a rarity that is until I started to
hear from other churches. Part of my job is to run the
New Life School of Worship, which means I get to train
worship leaders for local churches. We have a place on
our Web site where other churches can post their job
opportunities or needs. The list is available only to our
students and alumni to help them find a place to serve
when they graduate. I've been amazed to learn how
many churches find themselves in need of a worship
leader every few years. It's almost as if people jump
into full-time church ministry, and when they don't see
instant "revival" or growth or prominence, they leave.
Some even give up on church ministry altogether.

But maybe what's worse than giving up is the "success" of creating fast change and feeling confident that
we've made a lasting difference. Satisfied, we sit back
and revel in our accomplishments, when in reality the
change proves momentary and things soon return to
the way they were. We look at a church service, or
a conference packed with people, and call our job to
disciple others done. We sell books and CDs and convince ourselves that our calling to train people is being
accomplished. (Ouch! That hits close to home.) But sales
is not the same as impartation. An attendee is not a disciple. Mass communication doesn't automatically mean
personal transformation. But our obsession with quick
results and big numbers has blinded us to that truth.
Believing in instant change leaves us disillusioned, dor-
mant, or just plain deceived.

What fast change does do effectively is distract our
attention from our true work. We become convinced
that our own small, local change is so slow that it could

never truly accomplish anything. Our plodding routine could never compete with sensational sights. And so our gaze is drawn to the persistent flash of the "next great thing," and the light it casts makes our own work look dull and trivial to us, like shabby, old shoes not worth running in anymore.

GOD'S SLOW COOKING

Our fireworks approach to "making an impact" stems from a misguided quest for personal achievement. The drive to do something that matters, to be significant, leads us to a frenzied pace of activity.

Stop and watch people in a downtown city square. Everybody's moving. Cell phones glued to their ears, laptops on the subway—everybody's working. The current role they have isn't good enough. It's just a stepping-stone. And if the job they have proves to be a dead end, they'll quit and try something else.

We live like nomads in a suburban wilderness, moving from one thing to the next as if permanence were some sort of vice.

We live like nomads in a suburban wilderness, moving from one thing to the next as if permanence were some sort of vice. The average American changes jobs every eighteen months before the age of thirty-five.

And the situation improves only slightly after thirty-five. Then we stay for a mere three years. Most people have anywhere from three to five different careers in their lifetime. Is this because we're lousy workers and keep getting fired? Maybe it's that we are never satisfied. Maybe we view every season or situation as a short stopping point on the road to greatness.

Maybe deep down we're convinced that more money will make for a better life (or we'd at least like to find out for ourselves). We believe that a job title or a prestigious position is life's gold medal. We're no longer seeking to improve society or give back to the world or leave a mark, only to gain as much as we can before we leave. The world is a stage to be captivated and captured, not a vineyard to be cultivated and kept.

The drive to succeed is not necessarily the problem. It's the road we choose to get there that will make us or break us. How we define success determines our approach. We're enamored by the brilliant but momentary flash because we count success by the scope of influence or the scale of our efforts. But that's not how God defines success. We need to see our work not in the sporadic sparks of human achievements but in the steady light of God's eternal standards. As long as we use a worldly measure of success, our own work will likely be graded somewhere between poor and insignificant. But heaven's yardstick is not primarily about influence or numbers; it is first about faithfulness. It's not necessarily how much we do but that we do it, and keep doing it. God doesn't measure us by the list of our accomplishments, but by our faithfulness to the work he's given us.

In the unwavering light of Scripture, we learn something else about God's way of doing things. Oswald Chambers called it "the enormous leisure of God."[1] In simpler words, God is slow. The story of God's work in history is an unhurried, gradually unfolding tale. That's why the Old Testament is so long. Creation and Scripture bear witness to God's enduring slowness. There's nothing fast about the way an evergreen tree grows, or the way day fades into night. Even the miracle of human life takes roughly forty weeks from conception to birth— and then the rest of life is just beginning. God reminds us daily that his most beautiful charms are the ones that take time to develop. There is no quick way to become someone's friend or build a lasting marriage. The best things in life take time. The journey to the Promised Land lasted forty years; the Exile lasted seventy. From the time of Malachi, the last recorded Old Testament prophet, to the arrival of John the Baptist, nearly four hundred years elapsed. Christ's preparation for ministry took thirty years. But God is not slow "as some understand slowness," Peter reminds us. "He is patient . . . not wanting anyone to perish, but everyone to come to repentance."[2] God's work unfolds slowly, and good things are worth waiting for. But in our lives of instant gratification, the only thing we're slow about is learning God's ways.

PASSION, VISION, STRATEGY, FOCUS

For Nehemiah, the time came to leave his post as faithful cupbearer to the king and journey to Jerusalem to rebuild its walls. He went with the king's blessing and provision.[3] When he finally arrived in Jerusalem,

There is no quick way to become someone's friend or build a lasting marriage. The best things in life take time.

he took a few days to soak it all up. As passionate as Nehemiah was, he did not allow emotion to dictate his schedule. He hadn't begun this enterprise on a whim, and he wasn't about to carry it out on one. Three days after arriving in Jerusalem, Nehemiah slipped out under cover of darkness, inspected the state of the city's walls, and developed a strategy for restoring them. Then he met with the civic leaders.

"You know very well what trouble we are in," he began. "Jerusalem lies in ruins, and its gates have been destroyed by fire. Let us rebuild the wall of Jerusalem and end this disgrace!"[4]

The leaders were unified with hope and expectation. "Yes, let's rebuild the wall!"[5] Their mission was clear. Nehemiah's burning heart of purpose had begun beating in their chests. They were filled with his passion and on board with his strategy.

The people embraced the vision too, from every stratum of society, taking their places at the wall. Priests, goldsmiths, merchants, perfume makers, even district leaders, halted their regular business and worked on small sections of the wall or built a gate or hung its doors. Fathers and sons, grandfathers and grandsons, rich and poor, warriors, merchants and farmers, all became construction workers, family by family, each with small tasks to rebuild the giant wall.

I imagine myself there, listening to Nehemiah's impassioned speech about the disgrace of the Jews, about our city that lies in ruins. I feel my own heart burning within my chest. "Yes!" I shout with the crowd. "I will give my life! I will change the nation of Judah! I will restore this city!"

I see the people around me inspired by Nehemiah's vision. I sense the electricity of emotion buzzing through the crowd. And yet I watch Nehemiah unconcerned with maintaining that moment of passion. He doesn't ask the people to repeat a prayer, take a vow, or put wristbands on to spell out their devotion. Instead, he does something quite odd. He hands out *hammers*. Shocked, I hear him giving directions: "Build the Dung Gate. Stay there until it's done." "Rebuild this section of the wall. Let me know when you have it to at least half its finished height." I imagine myself stumbling over phrases in my head, wanting to say to Nehemiah, "But . . . I want to change the nation. I want to be the hope of the city. I think you might have misheard me. I said I wanted to be great, not that I would build a gate."

But the people who responded to Nehemiah didn't think twice about taking a post along the wall, devoting weeks on end to rebuild a single section. They understood that in order to accomplish this great task, they each had to faithfully work on their part—they had to *stay* until it was done.

God's enduring work doesn't happen on the high peaks of passion but in the flatlands of perseverance. Nehemiah and the people knew that mere excitement

God's enduring work doesn't happen on the high peaks of passion but in the flatlands of perseverance.

for the dream wasn't going to rebuild that wall. It would be sweat and blood and hard work that would do it. How is the wall of a great city built? By each one building a gate, hanging a door, laying a brick, swinging an ax, pounding a hammer. The building of a city or a nation may be commemorated by fireworks, but the actual work is done in the trenches. It's long days and dark nights of hard work. Burning hearts didn't rebuild the walls of Jerusalem; blistered hands and tired backs did.

The same is true for us today. Burning hearts for lost souls don't make anything happen; but hands used to make a meal, build a shed, clean a home, or wash some feet are doing "the good work that God has prepared in advance for us to do."[6] God's work is being done to change the world. But it is being done by followers of Christ, here and there, who do the small things and do them faithfully and persistently. The church in rural India, the school in Mississippi, the village in Uganda, the orphanage in Romania, the business in Iowa, the factory in China—these are all sections of the wall where God's workers are placed. And as we do the work, God himself is building his kingdom, the New Jerusalem. The work God has given each of us is aimed toward bringing new citizens into the city of God. If we refuse

to build our part of the wall, someone else will do it
and we will have no part in the greatness of that work.
Lasting change doesn't happen in the blink of an eye
or a thousand beats of the heart. Lasting change is the
result of faithfully working where you are, creating
small change over a long period of time. This is the third
secret of lasting change: Change is gradual.

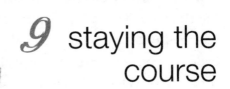

9 staying the course

Because lasting change unfolds gradually, it is paramount that we learn to stay. We must stay with a task until it's finished, or until God says we're done.

Undistracted faithfulness over the long haul is driven by both seeing the goal ahead and doing the task at hand. Staying focused on the goal helps us not to lose heart in the flatlands or in the darkness. Staying focused on the task ensures that we finish what we've started, or take it as far as God has asked us to.

Staying, in a geographic sense, also matters, because when we stay, God stays. Because God dwells in us and commissions us to do his good work, wherever we go, he goes. When we walk into a hospital room to visit the sick, God is there. He is there in more than just an omnipresent sense. He is there personally, in much the same way he was present on earth through Jesus Christ. We are not the begotten Son of God, but we are his children, and he has chosen to dwell in us and work through us. Jesus, in the fullest sense, was God on earth, Immanuel. When Jesus ascended to heaven, he promised to send the Holy Spirit. The Holy Spirit is God inside everyone who has agreed to represent him. The way that God is present on the earth in a special and specific way is through us. What a thought!

As Christians, we become God's men or women on the inside, like spies on a covert operation. As long as we stay "on mission," God has an agent on the scene. We're his hands and feet, on location, doing what needs to be done.

THE CHURCH THAT WOULD NOT LEAVE

The church of the early centuries is a shining example of what God can do when his people stay on the scene.

In the mid-second century, and again in the mid-third century, devastating epidemics hit cities throughout the Roman Empire. According to some estimates—using contemporary models and ancient records—fully a third of the Empire's population was destroyed. The diseases were most likely smallpox and measles.

We now know that a person who receives basic care—food, water, and other necessities—is capable of surviving smallpox, but at the time, the devastating effects of the epidemic sent panic throughout the affected regions. Even Galen, the famous physician who lived through the first epidemic, fled the city for the countryside for fear of contracting the highly contagious disease. In the cities that were affected, bodies were later found piled atop each other inside pagan temples, or strewn around the fountain in the city square. The sick had no one who stayed behind to care for them.

One could hardly blame the pagans for fleeing. No pagan religion at the time taught anything remotely close to an ethic of love or compassion. Their interactions with the gods were transactions based on personal gain. The deities desired human worship, and the people sought divine protection from particular disasters. It was a neat little arrangement, with no love or personal sacrifice involved. But when disaster struck, the pagans had no moral framework for caring for others.

Christians, on the other hand, believed in a God who had given his Son's life as a sacrifice for their sin. Their God loved them so much that he did whatever was necessary on his side to bridge the gap. Moreover, Christians were taught that God loved all human beings, not just those who loved him. He wanted Christians to love others just as he loved them. This love for others, in fact, was proof of their Christianity. It was their defining trait.

When the epidemics hit, the Christians were poised for success. Their faith offered hope of another, better world. The pagans had no explanation for calamity, and no reason for hope in the midst of it. The pagans fled for their lives or died alone. The Christians stayed and cared for their fellow believers who had contracted the disease. As a result, Christians had a survival rate far superior to that of the pagans. Because the Christians were closely connected, those who contracted the disease were immediately surrounded by believers who cared for them. The pagans more often found themselves abandoned by their friends, left to die or to fend for themselves.

Once a person survives smallpox, he or she becomes immune to it. We take this for granted, but it was not common knowledge at that time. As the Christians survived the epidemic and recovered, many of them returned to the affected cities and set up nursing camps to care for the sick.

God used acts of faithful Christian love to supernaturally expand his kingdom.

Imagine being a pagan at that time and having a group of Christians come to care for you—apparently unaffected by the disease! How could you not at least consider believing in the Christian God? His followers showed unprecedented sacrificial love, and some were even shielded from the deadly epidemic. God used acts of faithful Christian love to supernaturally expand his kingdom.

The eminent sociologist Rodney Stark suggests that
the Christian response to the epidemics was a major reason for the exponential growth of Christianity during
the second and third centuries. In his scholarly work
The Rise of Christianity, Stark maintains that the ratio
of Christians to pagans dramatically changed after the
epidemics. Because the Christians stayed on the scene
during the times of crisis, and because they "loved their
neighbors," Christianity flourished like never before.
Lasting change takes root when faithful people stay
where God has placed them.

OUTBREAK

I heard a story recently that remarkably resembles the
testimony of the Christians in the early centuries who
stayed in the midst of the epidemics. It's a story of
Christians in China who were unmoved in the face of
crisis and as a result, shone the steady light of God's love
to the lost people around them. This story also begins
with an outbreak.

On February 21, 2003, a sixty-three-year-old doctor from mainland China checked in to one of the 487
rooms at the Metropole Hotel in the heart of Kowloon,
Hong Kong. Days earlier, he had been in the Guangdong
Province of China, treating some cases of a strange
new virus. When he arrived at the Metropole, he had a
cough and other symptoms of a severe cold. By the time
he checked out, his ailment had infected at least eight
others in the hotel, some from other countries. One of
the eight was a twenty-seven-year-old man who stayed
on the same floor as the Chinese doctor. He was quickly
admitted to the Prince of Wales Hospital in Hong Kong,

where a large number of hospital workers caught the virus while attempting to treat him. Another guest of the Metropole that week was a young lady on her way to Singapore. Upon her arrival in Singapore, she was taken to the Tan Tock Seng Hospital, coughing, sneezing, and spreading the virus. Less than two weeks after he checked in to the Metropole, the Chinese doctor was dead.

An American businessman named Johnny Chen also stayed at the Hong Kong Metropole that week. A few days later, on a flight to Singapore, he suddenly came down with pneumonia-like symptoms. The plane made an emergency landing in Hanoi, Vietnam, so that Chen could be treated, but the treatment was unsuccessful. Chen returned to Hong Kong and died shortly thereafter. Within a few days, several of the doctors and nurses who had cared for him in Hanoi developed similar symptoms, and a few of them subsequently died.

On March 12, 2003, the World Health Organization issued a global alert regarding the virus—the first global warning in ten years. It would be another month before the disease would be named Severe Acute Respiratory Syndrome (SARS). It was known to be an atypical pneumonia caused by a brand-new virus called the SARS coronovirus. The initial death toll was not high enough to warrant widespread panic, but the ease and rapidity of its spread, uncertainty about its effects, and the lack of a cure were of grave concern.

In mid-March 2003, nine tourists aboard China Airlines flight 112, bound from Hong Kong to Beijing, caught the virus and perpetuated its international spread. Later that same month, a kidney patient from

the Prince of Wales hospital in Hong Kong was believed
to have ignited an outbreak when he visited his brother
in Block E of the Amoy Gardens apartment complex in
Hong Kong. Speculation about the virus swirled as sci-
entists and doctors contemplated "how a virus that is
usually transmitted by a simple cough or a sneeze [could]
infect hundreds of residents by raging through an apartment building with no central ventilation."[1] Could SARS
be completely airborne and spread by vapors from the
infected?

*The ambiguity of the
symptoms and the uncertainty
of the treatment fueled the
pandemonium.*

The ambiguity of the symptoms and the uncertainty
of the treatment fueled the pandemonium. Symptoms
such as fever, cough, sore throat, and gastrointestinal
discomfort typically do not indicate a life-threatening
disease. Some initial attempts to use steroids and other
antiviral vaccines proved to be detrimental. Antibiotics
did not work. To make matters even more confusing,
there were moments when the number of infections and
the number of deaths increased at different rates.

Health officials in Hong Kong scrambled to regain
control of the situation, implementing mandatory
screenings for anyone who had been in contact with an
infected person, and requiring all air travel passengers
to take a body temperature test to ensure they did not

have a fever when they boarded an airplane. In mid-April, the World Health Organization issued another health alert, confirming that the virus was being distributed globally via air travel. Globalization turned what would have been an isolated outbreak into a worldwide concern.[2]

PERFECT LOVE CASTS OUT ALL FEAR

As schools, theaters, and other entertainment centers in Asia began to shut down to prevent the spread of the virus, Chinese authorities believed that Beijing was becoming the worst-affected area in all of China, eclipsing even the Guangdong Province where the SARS virus first appeared.

Many foreigners in Beijing immediately plotted their exodus and left the country as quickly as they could, or sent their families home. Stores and restaurants resembled abandoned buildings as people stayed home. Hotels went from 90 percent occupancy to 15 percent. Beijing patients suspected of having SARS were allowed to be treated only in official government hospitals.

Dr. Larry Gee, an American family practice doctor, was living in Beijing with his wife and three children during the initial SARS outbreak. Dr. Gee and his friend Bryan Lee, an American marketing executive, saw the tremendous fear and knew they could not leave at a time like this. But they were not content to watch from the outside. They had to help somehow.

Under the auspices of the Beijing International Fellowship, the two men founded the Together SARS Support Center. Gathering more than two thousand volunteers from some sixty nations, they began to sup-

They were not content to watch from the outside. They had to help somehow.

port China's fight against SARS in several ways. They established a SARS information hotline, e-mailed a daily SARS informational newsletter, and helped to obtain and deliver medical supplies from abroad.

Perhaps the most helpful thing they did was also the simplest: They made care packages for their fellow health care workers. At the peak of the outbreak, hospital workers were required to work two full weeks without returning home. They were then quarantined for two additional weeks. If they showed no symptoms after that, they were allowed to return home to their families for two weeks. If all went well, they were away from home for four weeks, home for two, and then back on the front lines for another four weeks. Many were exhausted and emotionally drained, and received little support from their fearful friends and families.

Over the course of a few months, the group distributed 15,000 care packages to hospital workers and university students (many of whom were quarantined on their campuses to prevent the spread of SARS). The impact of these foreigners who had every right to leave but who chose to stay and demonstrate their tangible love and support was so great that their work was heralded on the front page of the *China Daily,* the Chinese government's primary English-language newspaper.

The paper quoted Bryan Lee, who had lived in Beijing for eight years, as saying, "Many left but we've stayed, for we saw the need. We believe that every crisis is an opportunity to learn and grow. All the volunteers are showing to the people of China that we care."

Dr. Gee echoed his friend's words: "We see the SARS epidemic as a way to deepen our commitment to serve, not as a reason to flee. . . . As a doctor, I came to China not only to work here but to serve the Chinese people." At no time was his commitment more evident than when he showed up at Ditan Hospital with his three young children to hand-deliver the first few care packages.

What value system creates such an ethic? What drove their commitment and made them dig in their heels and stay when so many others fled? Part of the answer is that the ones who assembled the care packages were all volunteers with Beijing's international Christian community.

The motto of the SARS Support Center was simply this: "Perfect love drives out fear." This reference to 1 John 4:18 was included as a central point in the *China Daily* article (but without the Bible reference).

It is still too early to tell the full impact of the Together SARS Support Center on the Chinese people, but the witness of their faithfulness and selflessness as they served the hospital workers and university students has been documented for decades to come. Those who received the care packages will never think about Christians in the same way again. Because the Christians courageously stayed when others left, God's light shone brightly in China.[3]

In May 2005, the World Health Organization

declared that SARS had been eradicated, making it only the second disease to have been given that designation. Interestingly, the other eradicated disease was small-pox—the very disesae whose devastation in the mid-second century was the backdrop for our other example of Christians who stayed and sacrificially cared for the sick.

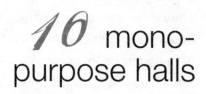

10 mono-purpose halls

I have a friend names James who rented a room in our house last year. We used to hang out together in our basement-turned-rec room and challenge each other's skills on my PS2. James recently spoke at a local Christian high school, using stories from his own experience to encourage the students to make wise choices in their teen years. As he was telling me about it later, he said, "Two classes of students combined, so we had to move the meeting into the cafetorium."

I couldn't help but interrupt, laughing. "The what? Where did you say you met?"

"In the cafetorium. It's a combination cafeteria and auditorium. A multipurpose room."

"That's what I thought you said."

Maybe you've been to a church that meets in an auditorium with hardwood floors and a basketball hoop pulled up into the rafters at either end; or a school whose gymnasium has linoleum tile floors, an attached kitchen, and a stage. Multipurpose halls are good for so many things and yet great for nothing in particular. They're an economical choice that satisfies multiple needs with equal mediocrity. It's not a great dining hall, because the room is usually stark and cold (though it can always be spruced up with greenery, a white lattice archway, and warm floor lamps for the annual couples' night out). If the floors are linoleum—or worse, car-peted—it's not a great basketball court; and with the high ceilings, it's a musician's nightmare venue. Many a band's career has suffered an early death in such a hall. Nevertheless, schools and churches keep building cafetoriums and basketball-court sanctuaries. For many organizations, economy is the highest virtue.

This multipurpose attitude filters into our choices of what to become a part of. We've become walking cafe-toriums, as if having our hands in several different pur-suits is better than excelling at one. Being well warned, we don't want to put all our eggs in one basket. We carefully guard against complete failure in one area by half-heartedly failing in several. But, being half-hearted, we don't feel intimately tied to our failure, so our pride is still intact when it happens. Even if we come up short in one pursuit, we're sufficiently diversified so that we haven't lost it all.

But isn't that exactly what Jesus called us to do—to lose it all? "Whoever loses his life for my sake will find it."[1] You can't follow God with a protective attitude. He demands recklessness. Since when did we stop trusting God when the possibility of complete failure exists? Or maybe it's the fear that if we've failed, we've let God down in some way. But remember, God doesn't define success or greatness the way we do. And he doesn't define failure the same way either.

> *God doesn't define success or greatness the way we do. And he doesn't define failure the same way either.*

Jesus didn't do his work half-heartedly. He was all in, all the time. He set the example that we are to follow. He set out "resolutely" toward Jerusalem, intent on dying and losing everything.[2] He did it precisely because he knew that losing it all meant finding it all at the end. At the point where the bitter cup of death was drunk to its dregs, there, in that moment, death itself was swallowed up too—in victory. Like Nehemiah, Jesus "wasted" his life bearing a cup. Like Jesus, Nehemiah knew that a life lost in God is eternal life gained.

The lasting change we're after unfolds gradually.

That's why it's imperative that we develop focus. Focus applies on two levels: duration and scope. Focus in terms of duration means developing the ability to give ourselves to something over the long haul, to be faithful, as we discussed in the previous chapters. Focus in terms of scope means narrowing the things we give our energies and efforts to—narrowing our attention to do the things that count, the things that matter.

The multipurpose life is a virtual death, because it's invested in nothing completely. The result of a life economically distributed among many different missions is one that doesn't leave a mark. We can do nothing well, or we can do one thing with all our might. And when we do one thing with our whole selves, something else happens. We stay. When we invest wholeheartedly in something, we stay to see it through. Lasting change is gradual. Lasting change takes time and a commitment to one thing.

When we invest wholeheartedly in something, we stay to see it through. Lasting change takes time and a commitment to one thing.

I know that the popular dysfunction of the day is Attention Deficit Disorder, but I don't think that we as a culture are really lacking in attention. It's not that we have a deficit, but that we have too many things competing for our attention. You know how I know?

Garage sales. As you walk through a typical garage sale, you wade past the normal kid stuff that the sellers have outgrown—swings, strollers, exersaucers, and a host of other molded plastic contraptions. But further inside the garage, behind the large plastic tubs of over-washed clothes, you'll find the garage sale's most ubiquitous item: the treadmill. Right beside it you're likely to find a set of skis and an old mountain bike with no visible signs of use. Garage sales are an airtight indictment of our lack of "stick-ability."

Innocent as it seems, distraction can be a death knell to accomplishing God-sized dreams. Clutter is the most successful adversary of purpose. When our lives are caught up with the appeal of new attractions, we're left with nothing to show for our good intentions.

THE PROMISE OF POWER

Billy Graham may have spoken in a few cafetoriums over the years, but his approach to ministry has never been multipurpose. The greatest evangelist of the last century has always had one goal: preaching the Good News of Christ's death and life. In the course of his life, Graham accomplished many great things, including preaching the gospel to more than two billion people. We could recite a list of his successes that would rival that of any world leader. The milestones and accomplishments in Billy Graham's life are well-documented. But what stands out to me are not all the people who heard a presentation of the gospel message through his ministry, as staggering as that number is. Nor is it all the opportunities he had, or the presidents and world leaders with whom he had an audience. What is most remarkable to me are not the things he *did;* it's all the things he *didn't do.*

He had the ear of every president in the latter half of the twentieth century, and connections that any politician would envy. But Billy Graham was not a politician, nor did he desire to be. His message and his purpose had digital clarity, and he kept it that way. Even when President Lyndon Johnson suggested he run for president and offered him a public endorsement and the assistance of his presidential staff, Graham brushed it off.

"Mr. President, I don't think I could do your job."

"Billy, I know you think I'm joking, but I'm serious. You're the man who might turn this country around."[3]

When the president of the United States offers you serious political clout and capital for the highest office of the land, in one of the greatest nations in the world, the open door to power and influence in such a position cannot be overstated. This was an opportunity to provide a positive influence and godly leadership to one of the most powerful countries on the planet! Such a prospect would have convinced lesser men that the offer was certainly God's will, indeed was their "calling." But Billy Graham understood that not every opportunity is God's open door. He turned it down and remained focused on his life's work. His certainty of purpose about his role in God's plan had to be rooted in something stronger than rock, steel, self, or faith—it had to be founded in God himself.

Graham's conversation with President Johnson wasn't his only brush with the prospect of political office. President Nixon offered him a number of high-ranking positions during his administration, and a Texas billionaire—perhaps assuming that money might

> *Billy Graham understood that not every opportunity is God's open door.*

speak louder than the promise of power—offered him $6 million if he would run for president.

Other offers were made that presented opportunities to influence the prevailing culture. For example, Paramount Pictures offered Graham a chance to capitalize on his charisma and good looks as an actor. And, in the late 1950s, NBC was willing to pay him "a million dollars a year to host a show opposite the highly popular Arthur Godfrey."[4]

Several friends and colleagues encouraged Graham to found a Christian graduate school, one that would rival the academic eminence of any Ivy League institution. This was something Billy Graham was interested in. He cared deeply about education and dreamed of seeing Christians respected for their intellect as well as their faith. At first, the pieces seemed to fall into place. Thousands of acres, along with millions of dollars, were pledged toward the cause. Graham University seemed destined to be. But it never happened. Billy Graham did not build a university, nor did he become an actor, or a TV host. He never ran for president or any other political office. He just preached. And preached. And preached.

STAYING PUT, STAYING FOCUSED

The people we consider great aren't typically ones who had their hands in many good causes. Rather, the ones who have had the greatest impact gave their lives with single-minded focus to one thing and were not distracted. They stayed focused and stayed put. They invested in one stock and did everything they could to make that stock pay dividends. Staying focused meant pursuing a narrow purpose. Staying put meant persevering over the long haul.

Nehemiah knew the importance of laser-like focus and perseverance. And his resolve was tested as he worked to rebuild Jerusalem's walls. He had two principal distractions, men named Sanballat and Tobiah. When Sanballat heard the news of Nehemiah's work on the walls of Jerusalem, he knew it would have political implications, that Jerusalem's status and power would be restored along with its walls. "What does this bunch of poor, feeble Jews think they're doing?" he mocked. "Do they think they can build the wall in a single day by just offering a few sacrifices? Do they actually think they can make something of stones from a rubbish heap—and charred ones at that?"[5]

Even Sanballat, the unmistakable villain of the story, knew what it took to create lasting change, and it wasn't a day's work and a few well-ordered sacrifices. He knew that it would require inspired people with able hands

They tried to dishearten the people by reminding them of how much work needed to be done.

and focused minds. In their efforts to distract Nehemiah and the people from their work, Sanballat and Tobiah attacked each of these aspects. They tried to dishearten the people of Jerusalem by reminding them of how much work needed to be done. The walls were just piles of broken stones, the gates simply bonfire ashes. But the people were not distracted. Sanballat and Tobiah called them feeble, unable to do the hard work of carrying rock and lifting it into place. They ridiculed the strength of the walls they were rebuilding, claiming that even a small fox could topple them. But the people were not distracted. Finally, these enemies threatened to attack and kill the people. "Before they know what's happening, we will swoop down on them and kill them and end their work."[6] Certainly, the fear of death would halt their work by distracting their focus. How do you stay focused when you're constantly checking over your shoulder for an ax murderer? You'd think they would be more concerned with defending their lives than building a wall. But the people were not distracted. They would not be stopped.

Nehemiah responded to the threats by posting guards, developing an attack-response plan, and arming everyone with swords. But Nehemiah wasn't consumed with reacting; he wasn't distracted from his main concern, and it wasn't a victory for Sanballat and friends. Rather, focused on the goal of restoring the wall, Nehemiah's response was measured to allow his priorities, the rebuilding, to continue. The distractions were dealt with summarily so that the focus could stay where it should. Even in Nehemiah's response, his single-mindedness was unmistakable.

Nehemiah's faith in God was his rallying cry. He reminded the people, "Don't be afraid of the enemy! Remember the Lord, who is great and glorious."[7] The perspective that drove Nehemiah to prayer when he first heard the news about Jerusalem was the same perspective he brought to the task at hand now.

The threats of their enemies served only to fortify the Jews' resolve. Then, Sanballat, Tobiah, and a third conspirator, Geshem the Arab, changed their tactics and aimed for Nehemiah himself. First, they attempted to flatter him by asking for a summit conference in a nearby town. They hinted at what a significant leader Nehemiah was, and how important a social figure he was becoming. But Nehemiah still would not be distracted. Four times they sent word, asking him to meet with them. Four times he sent the same response: "I am engaged in a great work, so I can't come."[8] He neither believed the flattery nor desired their praise. It was not fame he was after. He just wanted to stay put and stay focused.

I wonder if anyone who overheard Nehemiah's response might have leaned over to him and said, "Um, sir? That's not quite true. I mean . . . we're building a *wall*." Not exactly a textbook definition of a "great work." Nehemiah was not a prophet; he was not royalty. He had not killed a great enemy like David; he didn't play an instrument, or write a song. He never had a heavenly vision, like John, or a God-inspired dream, like Joseph; he never called down fire from heaven, or outran a chariot, like Elijah. He never parted a sea like Moses. Nehemiah, as far as we can tell, was an ordinary, unheroic man. His life's legacy was that he built a wall. And that was the high point. His résumé had two entries: cupbearer and construction foreman. And yet to Nehemiah, he was doing a great work.

Nehemiah's suspicion of his enemies' flattery proved to be on-target. He discovered that they had vowed to alert Nehemiah's old boss, the king of Persia, that Nehemiah was preparing to rebel, which was a slanderous lie. But even in the face of such potentially devastating slander, Nehemiah did not slow down. His assessment of the situation was simple and clear: "They were just trying to intimidate us, imagining that they could discourage us and stop the work." His resolve was equally lucid: "So I continued the work with even greater determination."[9]

> *People who create lasting change . . . stay the course, unhindered by the allure of fame or the threat of slander.*

That is the sort of focus, the kind of narrowness, we find in people who create lasting change. They stay the course, unhindered by the allure of fame or the threat of slander. They believe, deep in their hearts, that whatever their hands have found to do is a great work.

The distractions served only to steel Nehemiah's resolve. He had followed God too far to believe in his own greatness. He had already proven himself in his faithful, humble service to his oppressors. Nehemiah had prayed for God's power to open up opportunities, and he had walked through those open doors faithfully. His life of faithfulness had proven God faithful, a steady light on Nehemiah's path. The fireworks of his enemies could not distract his eyes from the goal.

11 multiplied efforts

Something powerful

happens when many people take up
the same cause. That's why the first thing
Nehemiah did after he surveyed the condition of the walls and gates of Jerusalem
was to recruit others to help rebuild the
wall. Nehemiah obviously had a special leadership quality that enabled
him to capture the imagination of
the people and get them to work

together in unison. Though he had been appointed as governor over the land, the authority of his leadership did not come from his title. It came from his passion and vision.

Perhaps above all, it came from his humility. He knew that building the wall would require more effort and energy than he could supply by himself. It would take an army. Nehemiah was a gifted man with immense favor from the Persian king, yet he refused to attempt the job alone. Building the wall was an urgent task, and there would be opposition. There would be those who would do everything in their power to stop the work, so Nehemiah needed help. He also realized that there were others who cared too. He was not so taken with himself that he thought he was the only true reformer.

When many people act in small ways for the same cause, right where they are, with the same faithfulness, over a long period of time, the impact becomes exponential. This is the fourth and final secret of creating lasting change: Change is exponential. It happens when we multiply ourselves, when we learn to work with others to harness the strength of diversity and numbers. We cannot be Lone Rangers. Rugged individualism and pride are not the hallmarks of successful change agents.

Lasting change happens when we learn to work with others to harness the strength of diversity and numbers.

Remembering that we are not alone in our quest
to create lasting change is a powerful thought; equally
potent is the conviction that it cannot be done alone.
Every history-shaping hero has had a faithful friend and
formidable sidekick. Nehemiah had Ezra, Luther had
Malanchthon, Washington had Nathanael Greene (among
others), Batman had Robin, Christ had his disciples, and
now his church—which means that we have each other.

UNITY IS NOT UNIFORMITY

God has chosen to do his work on earth through the
church. That is his way of perpetuating the Incarnation,
of reproducing himself, of multiplying his efforts.
Without knowing it, though, the church sometimes
obstructs his work, becoming a stone he has to work
around rather than a vessel he can flow through.

One of the chief ways that we become obstacles to
Christ's work is often disguised as a Christian virtue. It
stirs the emotions of tender and almost bleeding hearts
everywhere. It comes in the language of unity. No doubt
you've heard it:

> We should have just one main church, one main missions
> organization, with one person in charge, or a committee
> where everyone has a say.

> We don't need all these different ministries or organizations.

> We need a citywide rally where all the churches come
> together for a night of worship.

The list is long, but if you listen closely, the plea is
not truly for unity, but for uniformity. It is not for

collaboration, but for control. It is not for single-mind-edness, but for sameness. When unity comes to mean uniformity, it is no longer the answer. The diversity and dissimilarity of the body of Christ is not a weakness; it is its greatest strength. We don't all need to follow the same methods or the same human leader, or participate in the same program or campaign, in order to bring about lasting change. We don't even need to sing the same songs.

Diversity—whether applied to races, cultures, or ways of following Christ—is an idea that we love to talk about, but we have great difficulty actually embracing it. We like the way we are, and deep down, we wish that everyone else could be as wonderful as we are. It's one thing to choose our friends by the things we share in common. It's good to have a select few with whom we connect and walk through life. It's even better to be able to work with our friends. There is nothing like linking arms and working toward a common goal. If we are going to last, we have to have those kinds of people around us. But if we limit the spread of our cause to people just like us, we've missed the whole point of having others involved. When we look to advance Christ's work and create lasting change by reproducing ourselves, there is a strong temptation to clone ourselves. We tend to find people who are like us, or we try to persuade everyone else to adopt our methods and approaches.

OUT OF CONTROL

Both Luther and Nehemiah resisted such an urge, yet they both had large groups of people who took up their

*If we limit the spread of our
cause to people just like us,
we've missed the whole point
of having others involved.*

cause. For Luther, it was an army of reformers made up
mostly of people he had never met. As Luther's ideas
were disseminated through the written word, other people rallied to the cause. But Luther had never directly
addressed these people or personally recruited them. For
Nehemiah, the people shared his blood, his history, his
shame, and his passion. Yet the people who multiplied
both Luther's and Nehemiah's causes were of different
backgrounds and took different approaches from their
leaders. The bloody wars over theological minutia that
followed Luther's Reformation are horrid proof that not
all who believed in justification by grace through faith
in Christ had all things in common. Nehemiah's builders were a motley bunch from all walks of life. Some
who built the wall were priests and some were warriors.
Surely a warrior and a priest swing a hammer differ-
ently. The work each family accomplished at their section of the wall was not micromanaged. It was their section to own and to complete.

Luther and Nehemiah had different approaches to
the rapid multiplication of their efforts through others. Nehemiah gathered a strategic group of leaders and
painted a picture of how their lives had to be defined.
Luther could not control how other men would

respond after reading the truth of Scripture for the first time. Any attempt to do so would have made Luther into a new kind of pope, or central authority figure— the very thing he was trying to counteract. Even if he could have gained some sort of control, he would significantly have slowed the spread of Reformation ideas across Europe.

Nehemiah would never have built the wall without rallying the troops, daily keeping them focused, and even temporarily suspending normal economic practices of borrowing and lending to keep morale high. The change initiated by Luther took place on a massive scale and was creative, chaotic, and largely uncoordinated. Nehemiah's changes were focused and had a specific duration with a clear end. Despite their differences in leadership style, both Luther and Nehemiah achieved the same effect and had the same core philosophy. They reproduced themselves and multiplied their efforts by decentralizing control. They were willing to let go so that others could grab on. They didn't own all the shares; there was room for others to buy in.

The strength of diversity is only fully seen when control is decentralized. James Surowiecki elaborates on the brilliance of decentralized decision-making and problem-solving in *The Wisdom of Crowds*. He defines decentralization as a system, organization, or company in which "power does not fully reside in one central location, and many of the important decisions are made by individuals based on their own local and specific knowledge rather than by an omniscient or farseeing planner."[1]

Two important benefits immediately surface. First,

When individuals narrow their scope and become better at specific tasks, the group as a whole becomes more knowledgeable, efficient, and productive.

decentralizing "fosters, and in turn is fed by, specialization—of labor, interest, attention."[2] When individuals narrow their scope and become better at specific tasks, the group as a whole becomes more knowledgeable, efficient, and productive. Decentralization also creates the potential for increasing the diversity of opinions and information; there can be as many approaches and perspectives as there are people within the system. This leads to a second benefit, which economist Friedrich Hayek described as "tacit knowledge."[3] Surowiecki explains:

> Tacit knowledge . . . can't easily be summarized or conveyed to others, because it is specific to a particular place or job or experience, but it is nonetheless tremendously valuable. . . .
>
> Connected with this is the assumption that is at the heart of decentralization, namely, that the closer a person is to a problem, the more likely he or she is to have a good solution to it. This practice dates back to ancient Athens, where decisions about local

festivals were left up to the *demes,* as opposed to
the Athenian assembly, and regional magistrates
handled most nonserious crimes. It can also be seen
in Exodus, where Moses' father-in-law counseled
him to judge only in "great matter[s]" and to leave all
other decisions to local rulers. . . .

Decentralization's greatest strength is that it
encourages independence and specialization on
the one hand while still allowing people to coordi-
nate their activities and solve difficult problems on
the other. Decentralization's greatest weakness is
that there's no guarantee that valuable information
which is uncovered in one part of the system will
find its way through the rest of the system. . . . What
you'd like is a way for individuals to specialize and to
acquire local knowledge—which increases the total
amount of information available in the system—while
also being able to aggregate that local knowledge
and private information into a collective whole, much
as Google relies on the local knowledge of millions of
Web-page operators to make Google searches ever-
smarter and ever-quicker.[4]

Releasing control and empowering individuals allows a
system or a cause to harness the power of each individual's specialization and tacit knowledge. You could say,
then, that the test of our belief in the blessing of diversity is in our willingness to let others lead, work, and
use their uniqueness for the cause.

DISCIPLESHIP IN THE (FREE) MARKETPLACE

When I think of an example of empowering others to

lead, I need look no further than the church where I work. With such a large congregation, it would be easy for the church to function like a cold, slick corporation. The larger the group, the more disconnected the people become, and the more distant the leadership becomes from the rest of the group. We could sit in our executive staff meetings and develop a slew of ultra-cool programs based on surveys and demographic reports. We could form dream teams to imagine what that elusive and imaginary "ordinary congregant" wants and needs. Instead, our leaders developed a concept we call "Free Market Small Groups."

The larger the group, the more disconnected the people become, and the more distant the leadership becomes from the rest of the group.

The basic premise of Free Market Small Groups is that discipleship happens in the context of relationships, and relationships form around common interests, purpose, stages of life, and so forth. We have three semesters for our groups. Before each semester begins, potential leaders are asked to complete a simple application process. Once their application has been approved by the church's leadership, small group leaders can form a group on anything from Monday Night Football to an in-depth study of the book of Romans.

I do much of my pastoral work with twentysome-things, through New Life's college minstry, called theMILL. This ministry has spawned dozens of Free Market Small Groups, many of which involve some sort of outdoor Colorado adventure, such as hiking all the mountains over 14,000 feet in the Rockies. That's why I had to at least attempt some of these activities when I first moved to Colorado—to gain some credibility. But my efforts largely backfired. I am now notorious as the guy whose legs got so weary of snow-plowing down Breckenridge's lofty slopes that he actually rode the chair lift down the mountain and spent the rest of the day in the lodge with a book.

Each small group semester lasts for about twelve to fifteen weeks, so the people who decide to join a group only have to commit for a manageable length of time. They aren't forced into long-term relationships or commitments; they can take their time to let relationships form naturally.

A GRAND, INVISIBLE KINGDOM

Jesus designed the church to function as a diverse, fluid group that adapts to its host culture while maintaining its beliefs. It flexes but never folds. The five-hundred-year period following the New Testament era is a stunning example of the durability and grandeur of this design. During those years, Christianity experienced unprecedented growth and change.

James White, professor of liturgy at Notre Dame, expresses it perfectly: "From small cells of devout folk meeting in secrecy to vast crowds of the populace worshipping in imperial basilicas, Christianity went within a century from being the object of persecution to the official religion of the empire."[5] From a religion that began on the eastern fringe of the Mediterranean and remained there for several decades, it spread throughout the Roman Empire, including the lands west of the Rhine and the Danube rivers. In this same period, it crossed the sea, eventually spanning from Ireland to Persia, and multiplying its original geographical scope many times over. White continues with these important words: "This growth brought a wide variety of peoples of different cultures and languages to allegiance to Jesus Christ. All these peoples developed distinctive forms of worship, contributing their own cultural characteristics, yet preserving an essential unity."[6]

Distinct, yet one, there is evidence of their own cultural influence, yet proof of their essential unity. These descriptions also speak of what happens to us as individuals when we become Christians. With our own personalities, perspectives, and abilities, we are uniquely designed by Christ. When we come to follow Christ, we die to our own will and desires, and come alive to the life God designed for us to live. That's why Jesus said, "If you let your life go, you will save it."[7] We become the best and truest versions of ourselves when we are born again in Christ. That is to say, we become who we were made to be. Rather than losing our uniqueness and becoming amorphous redeemed souls, we become most fully the beings that God originally designed.[8]

But there's more. Each unique and fully alive being is held together in Christ.[9] Like bits of glass with each shard uniquely shaped and stained, the redeemed are brought together in a beautiful picture of Christ that,

*Like bits of glass with each
shard uniquely shaped
and stained, the redeemed
are brought together in a
beautiful picture of Christ
that brilliantly displays
his majesty.*

when illuminated by light, brilliantly displays his majesty. Here's how the apostle Peter puts it: "You are coming to Christ, who is the living cornerstone of God's temple. He was rejected by people, but he was chosen by God for great honor. And you are living stones that God is building into his spiritual temple."[10]

The temple, where God has chosen to live, is in us—collectively. As individual followers of Christ, our bodies are temples of the Holy Spirit who lives in us.[11] But Paul also emphasizes that collectively we are God's dwelling place: "Don't you realize that all of you together are the temple of God and that the Spirit of God lives in you?"[12]

The implications are tremendous. The revelation and manifestation of God's presence is not given to one super-believer or gifted leader. It is given to all of us *together.* Each of us, with our diverse expressions of *biblical* faith, carries a measure or an aspect of God's personality and presence. (I emphasize *biblical* because I am not advocating a subjective Christianity with no sense of doctrine or truth except that which is relative to each one's existential faith.) God is seen in each of us, and seen fully in the aggregate historical, universal church.

No Christian can be outside the church. It isn't an option to follow Christ while declining to be part of his body. Choosing which parts of Christianity we fancy is not a new phenomenon, but it has never been right in any era. In this age of increasing independence, we are drawn away by the mistaken notion that we can follow Christ but deny the church. This hinders Christ's work on earth, because no such choice exists. Paul made this clear to the rowdy Corinthians:

> The human body has many parts, but the many parts make up one whole body. So it is with the body of Christ. Some of us are Jews, some are Gentiles, some are slaves, and some are free. But we have all been baptized into one body by one Spirit, and we all share the same Spirit. Yes, the body has many different parts, not just one part.[13]

We have been baptized into one body. When we abandon our self-directed life and decide to follow Christ wholly, we join a grand, invisible kingdom that has been advancing for centuries. We become members of that great and glorious body that has been growing against all odds in every age and environment. There is no option for a "just Jesus-and-me" Christianity. Christ has a purpose that he plans to accomplish through his church. We are many and diverse. We have different stations at the wall—now with a hammer, now with a sword—all working together to build up the body of Christ.

To say that you love Christ and yet curse or disdain the church is to be fully ignorant of Christ.

The body of Christ has endured persecution and affliction; it has been imperialized and politicized, and yet it has survived. It began with a handful of followers and has grown to include members of virtually every race and culture. It is undeniable and unstoppable; it is majestic and yet feeble; glorious but still human. It is the original dream of God, and it remains so to this day. To say that you love Christ and yet curse or disdain the church is to be fully ignorant of Christ. It is just as foolish as bruising your eye to prove your independence. To know Christ is to love his church. To be a Christian is to embrace the church. Anything short of that is evidence of an immature and incomplete faith.

John the apostle spells it out repeatedly in his first letter:

> Dear friends, let us continue to love one another, for love comes from God. Anyone who loves is a child of God and knows God. But anyone who does not love does not know God, for God is love.[14]

> No one has ever seen God. But if we love each other, God lives in us, and his love is brought to full expression in us.[15]

If someone says, "I love God," but hates a Christian
brother or sister, that person is a liar; for if we don't
love people we can see, how can we love God,
whom we cannot see? And he has given us this
command: Those who love God must also love their
Christian brothers and sisters.[16]

We are not lone reformers or solitary revolutionaries. We
are builders in the work that Christ began. We are the
work and the workers. As Paul writes, "We are God's
workmanship, created in Christ Jesus to do good works,
which God prepared in advance for us to do."[17] We are
his work, made to do his work, and we must never forget it. We cannot deny the body of Christ its greatest
strength by refusing diversity and clinging to control
(if we do, we're just control freaks), and we cannot deny
Christ by trying to serve God outside of his body, the
church. We can no more do that than we can live outside
our own bodies. As for me, I want to be a part of God's
grand, invisible kingdom, held together by the power
of the Holy Spirit, and multiplying our efforts to accomplish God's purpose in the world.

12 love and war

There's one element that undergirds all our efforts to create lasting change: love. The apostle Paul makes it abundantly clear in 1 Corinthians 13:1-3 that all our achievements count for nothing if we don't have love. Oh, we can accomplish a lot without love, but nothing that matters for eternity. So, to talk about lasting change without also talking about love, is not just separating the cart from the horse, it's decapitating the horse.

Paul mentions three enduring virtues: "faith, hope, and love—and the greatest of these is love."[1] We need faith to ground us, hope to push us forward, and love to give our lives meaning. Faith believes in unseen things as if they were visible. Hope helps us to persevere, because we know that this world is not the end of everything. Love is the eternal virtue that God uses to describe his own essence. Without love, the greatest actions and achievements mean nothing. Without love, the grandest displays of faith and hope ring hollow and give way to despair and cynicism.

Leo Tolstoy, the great Russian novelist, paints a vivid portrait of a life without love:

> And what of it? I haven't stopped thinking about death," said Levin. "It's true that it's time to die. And that everything is nonsense. I'll tell you truly: I value my thought and my work terribly, but in essence— think about it—this whole world of ours is just a bit of mildew that grew over a tiny planet. And we think we can have something great—thoughts, deeds! They're all grains of sand."[2]

Levin is the melancholy, lovesick farmer/philosopher in Tolstoy's classic *Anna Karenina*. Kitty Shcherbatsky is the most flawless creature he has ever met. For Levin, nothing compares with her superior spirit and beauty. He once asked for Kitty's hand in marriage but was turned down because she was hoping for a proposal from the more socially acceptable Count Vronsky.

Then, in a later chapter, Tolstoy writes of Levin:

> He had not eaten for a whole day, had not slept for
> two nights, had spent several hours undressed in
> the freezing cold, yet felt not only fresh and healthy
> as never before but completely independent of his
> body. He moved without any muscular effort and felt
> he could do anything. He was certain that he could
> fly into the air or lift up the corner of the house if
> need be.[3]

What happened to death's appeal? Why this sudden
charge of energy and optimism? The only thing that
changed for Levin was that Kitty had realized the foolishness of her ways and had given herself fully to him.
His world opened up at that moment.

Toward the end of the great novel, when his life is
incredibly rich with love, Levin reflects, "Reason could
not discover love for the other, because it's unreasonable."[4] Ah, yes. Love is unreasonable.

SLAYING THE CYNIC

Reason does not give life to love—love gives reason to
life. Without love, there is no reason to believe, hope,
act, long for, or dream. People who don't believe in
miracles quickly change their minds when they or someone they love needs one. Only the bond of love can take
a discussion from the realm of conjecture into concrete
reality with its full force of emotion. The theoretical
becomes tangible in the presence of love. A person who
sees life as a series of ideas to be analyzed, dissected,
and evaluated does not understand love. Abstraction is a
form of alienation.

People who don't believe in miracles quickly change their minds when they or someone they love needs one.

Love is the only thing strong enough to slay the dragon of cynicism, in whose wake lie many once-valiant knights. Love is the virtue we see in fairy tales, conquering all. We taste it in our human relationships, but human love is just a shadow of God's love, a clue, not the full solution. God's love can bring the cynic to life as a new creature. It's like the kiss that turns the frog into a prince, the beast into a king, or Konstantin Levin into a courageous man.

Love is at once the problem and the answer. Love makes us afraid because it makes us vulnerable, but it also takes away our fear when we are loved fully and completely. "There is no fear in love. But perfect love drives out fear, because fear has to do with punishment. The one who fears is not made perfect in love."[5] Our hearts must be overcome, fully engulfed in the perfect love of God before we can risk loving another person. This explains the apostle Paul's prayer for those under his influence:

And I pray that you, being rooted and established in love, may have power, together with all the saints, to grasp how wide and long and high and deep is the love of Christ, and to know this love that surpasses

knowledge—that you may be filled to the measure of
all the fullness of God.[6]

What better preparation could there be for changing
the world than to be filled with all the fullness of God?
God, the source of all life, is a community within himself—the mysterious Trinity of God the Father, God the
Son, and God the Spirit. To be filled with the fullness of
God is to be swept up into the loving communion that
has existed within the Trinity since before time began.

We are welcomed into this union because of Christ.
He came to take our place of suffering and death so that
we could share his eternal place of fellowship. This is
what Paul means when he writes that we "become partakers of the divine nature."[7] In God, we are loved fully
and concretely.

When Nehemiah first heard of the plight of
Jerusalem, his tears gave evidence of his motives. He
was not driven by dreams of greatness or a desire to be
a revolutionary; he was simply moved by love for his
people. He could not bear the disgrace that covered his
people, and he wanted to help them. Before, he had only
imagined the worst about Jerusalem's condition; now,
there was no hope in ignorance. The truth had been told
in all its starkness, and his love for his people required
him to do something.

LOVING THE WORLD, HATING OUR NEIGHBOR

It is not enough to say that we have love. Many would-
be reformers of society have claimed a great love for
humanity, but their lives tell a different story. Take,
for example, the great nineteenth century English poet

Percy Bysshe Shelley. Shelley believed that poets were the "unacknowledged legislators of the world" and that poetry could "push forward the moral progress of civilization."[8] His poetry lived up to his own high expectations of the art, and most of his works were highly moral and political. He wrote of an uprising against oppression, of the freedom and equality of all human beings, and he imagined a mythical being "leading humanity to utopia on earth." He called his readers "to join him in his righteous utopia."[9]

Shelley's personal life, however, was littered with the casualties of the men and women who loved him but whom he eventually destroyed. He was estranged from both parents and his first marriage lasted only three years (producing two children) before he left his wife for another woman. After marrying his mistress, he had other sexual affairs, abandoned an illegitimate child, left his debts unpaid, and fleeced friends and family members for money.

In his sobering work, *Intellectuals,* Paul Johnson writes that Shelley was "capable of feeling for, in the abstract, the whole of suffering humanity, yet finding it manifestly impossible, not once but scores, hundreds of times, to penetrate imaginatively the minds and hearts of all those people with whom he had daily dealings."[10] Johnson is a fan of Shelley's poetry, but he summarizes Shelley's life in this way:

> Shelley [was] astonishingly single-minded in the pursuit of his ideals but ruthless and even brutal in disposing of anyone who got in his way. Like Rousseau, he loved humanity in general but was often cruel to

human beings in particular. He burned with a fierce love but it was an abstract flame and the poor mortals who came near it were often scorched. He put ideas before people and his life is a testament to how heartless ideas can be.[11]

Shelley's life is not an anomaly. Many intellectuals who dreamed of shaping society and revolutionizing the world were famous for "loving humanity" but loving no actual human being. Karl Marx, whose Communist Manifesto was driven by his alleged love for the worker, knew only one member of the working class well: Helen Demuth, known as "Lenchen," his wife's servant. Marx had an affair and a child with her (a son, whom he never publicly acknowledged), and despite his concern for the working class, he never paid Lenchen a penny.[12] It's no wonder that Marx's theoretical society, when implemented by Lenin, Stalin, and Mao, created horrifying political regimes that resulted in the most catastrophic human casualties of modern history. If we are to create lasting change, we must not be reformers moved chiefly by ideas; we must be moved, as Christ was, by love—not for humanity in general, but for the people we know in particular.

It is impossible for us to love the world. Only God can accomplish this feat because he is able to be with every person simultaneously.

It is impossible for us to love the world. Only God can accomplish this feat—because he is able to be with every person simultaneously. We cannot love "the lost," or "humanity," or "our generation." We can only love the specific people who surround us at home, at work, or wherever we find ourselves. Loving "the world" is a great misunderstanding of Christianity that has deterred many from simple service and ordinary kindness to the people right in front of them. "Universal love" does not inspire meaningful action.

FIGHTING FOR WHAT YOU BELIEVE IN

A love that is specific and personal leads to a willingness to fight for the beloved. In American history, Valley Forge, a stretch of high ground above the Schuylkill River in eastern Pennsylvania, has become a symbol of courage and fortitude in the worst of situations. The motley crew of 12,000 men who gathered there in the early months of 1778—in truth, you could hardly call them soldiers—became the catalyst for the birth of a nation. Though most of them had never been in military service before, let alone participated in combat, by the time they marched to engage the British the following summer, they had been forged into a formidable military force.

Despite near starvation, a lack of discipline and organization, and the ravages of disease and winter weather, these men rallied behind their leaders—most notably George Washington and Nathanael Greene—and helped to turn the course of the Revolutionary War and lay the foundation for one of the greatest nations on the earth. Of course, not one of the men in that frigid val-

ley that winter knew that they would accomplish all
that, and it isn't what they set out to do. Initially, they
weren't even trying to create a nation. They were simply
fighting for their lives, and for the ordinary freedoms
they knew and loved. Farmers fought for their farms,
mill workers for their young enterprises, and everyone
for their families' safety and right to be represented. No
one was fighting for a place in history. Even Nathanael
Greene, the quartermaster general of the army at Valley
Forge, said, "I am determined to defend my rights and
maintain my freedom or sell my life in the attempt." He
was fighting for himself.

*They were fighting for their
lives, and for the lives of
the ones they loved, not for
some epic dream of a great
America.*

And that is the point. Everyone who fought in what
we now call the Revolutionary War was fighting for
what they knew and held dear. They fought for specific,
concrete reasons—hearth and home—not some tran-
scendent ideal, lofty concept, or world-changing goal.
There were some who spoke of a Grand Experiment, a
nation shaped by certain ideals, but most of that rheto-
ric was heard far from the battlefield. Almost none of
it came from General George Washington. Out on the
field, where many died of starvation, sickness, and cold,

in addition to those killed in combat, they were fighting for the right to live in their chosen way without the arbitrary interference of a government in which they had no say. They were fighting for their lives, and for the lives of the ones they loved, not for some epic dream of a great America. A love that is personal leads to a commitment that is costly.

A TIME FOR WAR

You may recall that at one point, the opposition against Nehemiah and his crew rose to such a frenzy that his enemies, Sanballat and Tobiah, began plotting a fight against the Jews. Wars have been fought over many things, and conflicts inflamed by the smallest acts. But has an international war ever been sparked by a nation rebuilding its own walls?

The workers were exhausted. They had been laboring relentlessly on the walls, yet the piles of rubble were so great that they had to have felt they were making no progress. You know the feeling: It's like when you're reading, replying, forwarding, and deleting your e-mails, but your inbox is still overflowing. Okay, so it's not like that. It's a lot worse. We're talking about moving burned wood and stone, the ruins of an entire city, out of the way, and building a new wall in its place. After clearing debris for days, it seemed as if they had not even begun. Morale was not high when news of an impending battle filtered into town.

"Before they know what's happening, we will swoop down on them and kill them and end their work," their enemies said.[13] Terror seized the hearts of the Jews living near the enemy. Afraid that they would be the first casualties of a brutal attack, they spread the alarm through the city: "They will come from all directions and attack us!"[14]

When Nehemiah heard the threats and saw the fear that ripped through Jerusalem like a wildfire, he knew he had to act quickly. He immediately stationed armed guards behind the lowest parts of the wall, where the city was most vulnerable. He had others stand with weapons to protect their families.

Then came the speech. As in every good Hollywood war epic, Nehemiah's story includes a pre-battle speech. He called the leaders and the people together and addressed them with a stirring oration that would have made William Wallace proud. Ron Howard couldn't have produced a better pull-your-heartstrings moment. "Don't be afraid of the enemy! Remember the LORD, who is great and glorious, and fight for your brothers, your sons, your daughters, your wives, and your homes!"[15]

Courage returned to their hearts, and purpose took the place of fear. Nehemiah took half of his men off the wall and commissioned them to stand guard with spears, shields, bows, and armor. He stationed officers behind the men who worked on the wall. The laborers did their work by carrying a load in one hand and a weapon in the other. The builders had swords strapped to their sides. A trumpeter was always at Nehemiah's side, ready to sound the alarm at a moment's notice. The instructions were made clear to the nobles: "The work is very spread out, and we are widely separated from each other along the wall. When you hear the blast of the trumpet, rush to wherever it is sounding. Then our God will fight for us!"[16]

TO WORK AND TO WAR

I wonder if anyone listening to Nehemiah's speech thought to himself, *"A weapon? That's not what I signed up for. I am a man of peace. I came to work, not to war."* The Jews had lived in captivity for some seventy years by that time. It is unlikely that any had ever been involved in combat. Even if they had learned to wield a sword or shoot an arrow, they probably had never tested their skills against a hostile foe. They knew stories of the legendary fighters in their history—Joshua, Samson, Gideon, David—but they did not know anyone who had slain a giant or conquered an army larger than theirs. They loved Jerusalem and wanted to rebuild its walls, but they probably weren't counting on bearing a sword and standing guard.

Nevertheless, these men and women did not shrink back in their hour of opportunity. They picked up their swords as willingly as they had picked up their hammers. They met the challenge with courage, a readiness to fight, and a willingness to die.

We might have answered the call to service because

> *They picked up their swords as willingly as they had picked up their hammers. They met the challenge with courage, a readiness to fight, and a willingness to die.*

of a desire to do God's work, to follow him as he shapes history, to play our part in his story and create lasting change. But there comes a time when God asks us to take up a sword and stand watch. Priests, farmers, merchants, and builders—some continued to work, others became sentinels, but even those who labored were ready to fight, for all had become soldiers. These are the moments when we are reminded that following Christ means denying ourselves, and that denying ourselves is not just theoretical. It must lead us to leave what is comfortable and risk our own safety, advancement, or desires. Creating lasting change as we follow Christ is not only about work; it is also about war.

War is not a popular subject these days, especially among Western nations. It seems that no cause merits bearing arms, and no freedom is important enough to die for. I am not pro-war for the sake of war, but I wonder if somewhere in our path to enlightened diplomacy we've lost the willingness to stand for something. I once heard a respected pastor at a meeting of influential denominational leaders say he "didn't like war metaphors." I wondered what he did with the Old Testament, or the war metaphors in Christ's speeches or Paul's letters.

Biblical war language does not justify political military crusades, but it is the basis for our engagement with the forces of darkness. There is an enemy. There is a good guy and a bad guy. The good guy is much bigger and stronger, and in fact, he has already won. But he wants us to take what is already his and be willing to fight for it. War is an inescapable part of the Christian journey. A statement like this would have been an exercise in redundancy even a few generations ago; but today, in the comfort of prosperity and the safety of the "moral majority," the skin of our souls has grown thin, and war metaphors make us squeamish. It cannot be this way.

If we love God, we will sacrifice our lives to serve him. If we love people, we will lay down our lives for them. Love makes our work meaningful. And when our work leads to war, love leads us into the battle.

13 the cost of change

Here's the unavoidable truth: Change is costly.

John the apostle had a vision toward the end of his life, a vivid portrayal of an epic battle between a dragon and those redeemed by the Lamb. It has all the elements of a blockbuster sci-fi movie. Toward the end of John's retelling of his vision, he gives the secret to how the redeemed ones overcame the dragon: "They have defeated him by the blood of the Lamb and by their testimony. And they did not love their lives so much that they were afraid to die."[1]

I understand the metaphor—mostly. I know that the dragon is a picture of Satan and his systems, embedded in a worldly order that organizes itself apart from God. I believe that overcoming the dragon by the blood of the Lamb means having our sins and the guilt and blame from those decisions washed away by the work of Jesus Christ on the cross. I know that it refers to repentance, turning away from one way of living and turning toward Christ. I understand that our "testimony" has to do with the fruit of repentance, proclaiming with our lives what Christ has done in us; it means that we become visible evidence of the transformation available only through Christ. But "they did not love their lives so much that they were afraid to die" has always been a little tricky. Being willing to die for Christ is not a common concept in twenty-first century American Christianity. Most of us have never come close to persecution, much less martyrdom. We have no grid for it, no way to digest such a concept, no file cabinet to categorize such a thought.

For the readers of John's written revelation, it was not a concept, but a reality. According to tradition, John had miraculously survived numerous attempts by Roman authorities to kill him for his faith. For many early Christians, being willing to die for Christ was not a virtue they aspired to, but part of the job description of being a believer. Every new convert knew that becoming a Christian could warrant a punishment of death by the Roman courts. There was little chance that one could become a Christian and still be "in love with yourself."

They weren't paying a cost to create lasting change; they were paying a cost because that's what following Christ entailed.

> *We plead with people to "accept Christ" as if he were some sort of social reject in need of friends.*

These days, the thought of dying for Christ is not even suggested when we call people to salvation. In fact, as my friend Brent Parsley, the youth pastor at our church, says, "We plead with people to 'accept Christ' as if he were some sort of social reject in need of friends." Christ is not someone to be "accepted," like a new trend, an awkward kid, or a set of freshly posed ideas. He is the Lord of all creation, to be obeyed; the Savior, to whom all faith is to be devoted; God himself, to whom all life returns in worship. A cost is inherent in the call to follow Christ. We understand the part of the cost that refers to denying our own sinful pleasures and desires. We grasp that, at least intellectually. But the part of the cost of following Christ that means a willingness to actually die for him seems a little absurd in our context.

What could dying possibly accomplish? Well, in Ecuador, in 1956, it opened the way for an entire tribe to be transformed. It sparked an incredible rise of interest in Christian missions among the youth of that time. Even today, the deaths of five young missionaries at the hands of the Waodani tribe is still considered the greatest inspiration to missionaries all over the world. Jim Elliot, Nate Saint, Pete Fleming, Ed McCully, and Roger Youderian acted within their reach and took an incredible first step. More than that, they gave themselves fully to their cause, not loving their lives, even unto death. Jim Elliot, perhaps the best known of the group because of his articulate journaling, wrote, "He is no fool who gives what he cannot keep to gain what he cannot lose." Another of his quotes reveals the secret behind the effectiveness of their mission: "Wherever you are, be all there. Live to the hilt every situation you believe to be the will of God." If you want to follow Christ as he shapes history, you have to give yourself fully to him. You have to be obedient to the task he gives, no matter the cost. Creating lasting change—Christ's way—means dying to yourself.

If you want to follow Christ as he shapes history, you have to give yourself fully to him.

A FAITH TO DIE FOR

By most estimations, Christianity experienced its most rapid and dramatic growth in the early centuries of the common era. Scholars and pastors have searched for ancient models and formulas that can easily be transplanted into today's world, but as church historian Justo Gonzáles points out, "The ancient church knew nothing of 'evangelistic services' or 'revivals.'"[2] Early Christian worship services centered on receiving Communion together, and only those who had been baptized were allowed to participate. Gonzales concludes that the only way for non-Christians to have been evangelized was for Christians to have witnessed to them in "kitchens, shops, and markets. . . . Most converts were made by anonymous Christians whose witness led others to their faith."[3]

The most powerful form of witnessing was one that demonstrated a particular quality of the early Christians, one that is still seen in many Christians around the world today: the willingness to die for their faith in Christ. The term *martyr* originally meant simply "a witness." The early martyrs were witnesses to the life and lordship of Jesus Christ and his power to save; they testified unflinchingly in the Roman courts, refusing to deny their faith in Christ or hail a pagan deity, even to the point of death. The witness of those who were put to death for their faith in Christ had an impact on early church growth that cannot be overstated.

"OUT WITH THE ATHEISTS!"

Polycarp, bishop of Smyrna in the second century, was just such a witness. He had been mentored by the great Ignatius, who was also martyred for his faith.

Trouble started brewing in Smyrna in AD 155, when a group of Christians were brought before the Roman authorities and ordered to worship the pagan gods. They refused. As punishment, they were fed to wild animals in the arena, while a crowd of Roman citizens watched. Rather than being shocked or disturbed by the carnage, the crowd began to chant with hysterical fury, "Bring us Polycarp!"

When word got out that the bishop's life was in danger, his followers urged him to hide. At first he resisted, but finally moved to an estate outside the city. Still, he could not hide forever. Finally, he decided that it must be the will of God for him to be martyred. With peaceful resolve, he awaited the arrival of the arresting officials.

When Polycarp was brought to trial, the presiding proconsul ordered him to yell, "Out with the atheists!" To the Romans in that day, the Christians were considered atheists because they did not worship a visible God. The idea of an invisible God was essentially no god at all. Instead of complying with the proconsul's demands, Polycarp turned to the crowd, pointing his bony finger at them, and said, "Yes, out with the atheists!"

"Polycarp! Listen to me," the proconsul implored. "If you will simply swear by our great emperor and curse your Christ, you will be free to go, free to live out the rest of your life in peace."

"For eighty-six years I have served him," Polycarp replied. "And he has done me no evil. How could I curse my king, who saved me?"[4]

Again the proconsul entreated Polycarp, and again Polycarp refused to swear allegiance to the emperor. At last, his patience spent, the proconsul resorted to threats. "Polycarp, if you don't stop this foolishness and do as you are told, I will burn you alive!"

"Even the hottest flame you could light could not compare to the great fires of hell!" Polycarp responded. "Yours will burn for but a moment; God's flames for all eternity."[5]

The crowd was stunned. The proconsul now had to prove that his threat was not idle. Polycarp was taken outside, yet even as the soldiers were about to nail him to the pyre, he refused to recant, saying that the conviction that held him to Christ would hold him amid the flames.[6] He lifted his head toward heaven and prayed with a loud voice: "Lord Sovereign God . . . I thank you that you have deemed me worthy of this moment, so that, jointly with your martyrs, I may share in the cup of Christ. . . . For this . . . I bless and glorify you. Amen."[7] The flames leapt from the ground, engulfing his body and carrying his soul to heaven.

In the story of Polycarp's death, one observer wrote that it was "not as burning flesh but as bread baking or gold and silver refined in a furnace."[8] The smell from the fire was the scent of a sweet offering made to God, for "precious in the sight of the LORD is the death of his saints."[9]

THE STEADY CALL TO FAITHFULNESS

When others see someone sacrifice for a belief, they are inspired to consider that belief more seriously. When they see others die for their beliefs, they can't help but examine the beliefs for which those people died. What could be so compelling that someone would be willing to die for it? When others see someone make a sacrifice apparently devoid of any personal benefit, they wonder, "What about that belief could be so valuable?"

Sociologist Rodney Stark puts the question this way: "Perhaps rational people are willing to give money and time to social service and observe strict norms governing sex and marriage because of religion. But how could a rational person accept grotesque torture and death in exchange for risky, intangible religious rewards?"[10] Yet it was the willingness of the early Christians to suffer horrific deaths for their faith in Christ that signaled a clear message to the pagans of their day: Christ must be something special.

> *How can belief in a nebulous idea like eternal life in an unknown, unseen place really compel us to give up everything to follow Christ?*

But even today, many believers echo Stark's question. How can belief in a nebulous idea like eternal life in an unknown, unseen place really compel us to give up everything to follow Christ? Being willing to die for our faith in Christ is not something that most Americans have encountered personally. Though we may be aware of fellow Christians around the world who are persecuted and suffering, most of us have never come close to persecution ourselves. Most have never been confronted at gunpoint, tortured, or barked at to denounce our faith.

Furthermore, for most of us, our commitment to Christ may never be tested by anything more than the prospect of social rejection. So the answer is easy, because the question is theoretical. But here's a harder question: Will we live in such a way that dying for

Christ becomes more probable? Will we put our lives
in danger when necessary in order to follow Christ and
advance his work? Will we sacrifice comforts and luxuries to follow Christ? In whatever situation God chooses
to put us, will we be faithful followers at all costs?

After living for more than eighty years, certainly
Polycarp had seen it all. He'd had his faith tested in dark
places, and had his dreams dashed by the steady call to
faithfulness. Yet that steady call to faithfulness proved
to him the faithfulness of God. He had persevered in
trusting God, and God had not let him down. Now,
as he faced the judgment of the proconsul, Polycarp
seemed certain that even death was not a failure of God's
faithfulness; that beyond death, God would prove faithful in rewarding Polycarp's faith.

It's interesting that Polycarp answered the proconsul's
demands with a question. "How could I curse my king,
who saved me?" He could have made it a statement: "I
will not curse the king who saved me." But as a question,
it reveals a number of things about Polycarp's faith. First,
he saw his death as part of his obligation to God. God had
graciously redeemed him from a path of destruction and
put him on a path to life. Thus, Polycarp's death could
not be seen as evidence of God's failure, but rather as
Polycarp's opportunity to respond to God's grace. Second,
his question reveals that he knew only one logical answer.
How *could* he curse his king? He couldn't. For all God
had done for Polycarp in his eight decades of life, for the
whole of Polycarp's experience in following him, only
an irrational man would have cursed God. Only a man
who had lost all grip on reality would have thought it
sensible to curse God in order to live. No, there was only

one rational conclusion: death. Finally, beyond the apparent obligation, more powerful than sheer reason, there was love. Deep in the question that Polycarp asked, you can hear his heart; he was asking himself the question as much as he was addressing the crowd or the proconsul: "How could I do such a thing? It would break my own heart to reject the truth of my love." Besides his other reasons, Polycarp was compelled by a love that manifests itself, that he could feel like his heartbeat, so much so that to curse God would've been to deny everything he knew about himself.

Many who heard Jesus' words found them too difficult to comprehend or obey, so they packed up and left.

"TO WHOM WOULD WE GO?"

When Jesus taught in the synagogue in Capernaum, he made many claims about himself that some of his followers found hard to understand and even harder to believe. It's not surprising when you consider some of the hard sayings of Christ, such as, "Anyone who eats my flesh and drinks my blood has eternal life."[11] Many who heard Jesus' words found them too difficult to comprehend or obey, so they packed up and left. Jesus then turned to those who stayed, the twelve disciples among them, and asked, "Are you also going to leave?" Peter, aware of his own obligation, logic, and love, responded, "Lord, to whom would we go? You have the words that give eternal life."[12] Indeed, there was no one else. No other name under heaven. Jesus was the only option for people who wanted a hope, an answer, a Savior. Only irrational people would pack up and leave, truly "curse God and die" in their sins. To whom would we go? We are bound to you. We can see no other choice besides you. We love you.

When we begin to know Jesus the way Polycarp did, the way Peter did after giving his life to follow him, after experiencing his abiding faithfulness and love toward us, we begin to understand the pleasure of sacrifice. We begin to see that *sacrifice* is merely a term used from an earthly perspective. There are moments in life when we catch a glimpse of the supreme value of knowing Jesus, of all the benefits we receive from loving him, and in those moments, the word *sacrifice* hardly passes our lips because we realize that to not know Jesus is the real sacrifice. When we begin to understand the truth about Jesus and his incomparable worth, to do anything but embrace him by giving up earthly treasures is the real sacrifice. To settle for anything less than Jesus himself is sacrifice. When we see Jesus for who he truly is, we can echo Paul's words: "I consider everything a loss compared to the surpassing greatness of knowing Christ Jesus" and "What we suffer now is nothing compared to the glory he will reveal to us later" and "Our present troubles are small and won't last very long. Yet they produce for us a glory that vastly outweighs them and will last forever!"[13]

A LESSON IN OBEDIENCE

My dad was a successful account executive for a New York-based ad agency. In their Malaysia office, he handled accounts for major corporations such as M&M Mars, Volvo, and De Beers. The job came with great perks, such as a company car, trips overseas, a country club membership, and—my favorite—large quantities of chocolate.

When I was ten years old, my dad quit his job. He and my mom had been praying for a while about going to America to learn more about the Bible and about what it meant to serve God in "full-time ministry." They loved teaching the Scriptures and counseling people. It was something they had begun doing simply to fill a need, but they quickly discovered that people were drawn to them. The timing seemed right. Their desire to spend more of their time mentoring and teaching people was met with growing evidence of God's blessing on it. Their leaders and their friends affirmed the decision to head to Bible college.

> *Their desire to spend of their time mentoring and teaching people was met with growing evidence of God's blessing on it.*

It's a good thing I was too young to recognize the craziness of their choice. Moving to America? Why not? I didn't think about how our Malaysian dollar would be worth only about a quarter in the U.S. I didn't really consider how we would earn any money with both my parents in school full-time. My older sister, Tracy, and

I—we were ready for an adventure, and the possibility
of a white Christmas.

When we arrived in Oregon, my dad got a job working as a janitor at the church that ran the college. We
bought an old Toyota station wagon for about $400. We
lived first in a duplex apartment and then later in a ten-
apartment complex we called "the tenplex." My parents
had enough money saved to pay for their tuition and a
few basic necessities. Most of the money my dad made
vacuuming the church hallways went to pay the rent
and buy groceries. There was little room for luxuries.

We had a bicycle that someone gave to us. To save
money on gas, my dad rode it to the grocery store about
ten blocks away. Tracy and I often walked along to help
carry the bags. One time, my dad went alone, and on the
return trip the grocery bags were too much to balance.
He lost control and ran into a wall. It was pretty sad.

One night, while sitting on our thrift store sofas,
we had a severe craving for pizza. We didn't have the
money to squander on Pizza Hut, so our longings had
to be satisfied by joking about sinking our teeth into a
cheesy pan pizza. When the doorbell interrupted our
playful misery, we ran to see who it was. On the door-
step stood one of our neighbors, holding a couple of
pizza boxes. He said he was having a party and had
overestimated his guests' appetites. Could we make use
of some leftover pizza?

As young as I was, I never thought of those years as
difficult. We were never unhappy. We had great times
in the kitchen, pitching in to cook and clean. We spent
Saturday mornings praying together, singing along with
our worship tapes, and reading the Bible. We talked

about everything in our lives. Those years forged a bond within my family that distance has not been able to dissolve.

As a parent myself now, I have a better idea of how hard it must have been for my mom and dad to leave their high-paying jobs and the familiar comforts of home to spend three years in a foreign country with their two children. They didn't know anyone in Oregon. In Malaysia, they were on top of the world, surrounded by friends who loved them, and my father's career was on the rise. They were experiencing success at every turn. What drove my parents to leave all that was not the search for a better life. It was not the immigrant's quest in the land of opportunity. It was obedience to God's call. Our move across the Pacific was a defining moment for our family. It was then that I understood that being a Packiam meant obeying God at all costs. As I watched my father trade his corporate career for an industrial vacuum cleaner, and his country club membership for cleanup duty, the lesson was etched on my heart: Nothing else matters except obedience.

It was only by our choosing to faithfully follow God that he could show us that he wouldn't steer us wrong.

It was my parents' example, not their words, that convinced me of this. Not only that they valued obeying God but that obeying God was the best choice to make.

Their decision to follow God each and every day proved itself out; God proved himself faithful in supplying what we needed. It was only through our obedience that God could do that. It was only by our choosing to faithfully follow him that he could show us that he wouldn't steer us wrong. Like Polycarp and the martyrs of old, my parents understood that their faithfulness to follow Christ would give God occasion to prove his own faithfulness. The question was whether we would bail out before we got there. My parents showed me how not to bail out.

Ultimately, creating lasting change requires a costly obedience—an obedience to the Director's leading, when he calls us into the spotlight for greatness, and when he calls us to step into the darkness. In either role, obedience means making sacrifices. But they are only sacrifices as long as we consider anything from the world to be more valuable than God himself. A sacrifice is hardly a sacrifice when love values the object gained to be greater than all. Love for God puts God first, and everything else grows dim by comparison, so that there is no sacrifice too great that love would not make. There is no sacrifice too small that love would ignore. Jesus showed it himself, washing his disciples' feet like a servant and dying a gritty death like a sinner. But he did it "for the joy set before him," knowing that he would rise to sit beside God in glory, knowing that by his sacrificial death he was opening the way for lasting change. To be a follower of Jesus, to love him and love others as he did, requires an obedience that will cost us our lives. When we are ready to die, we are ready to make a world of difference.

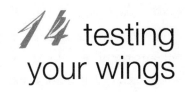

14 testing your wings

This is the story of a
friend, an extraordinary young man, who embodied all the principles we've been talking about for creating lasting change.

Ben Couch was one of those mountain types who shopped almost exclusively at REI and had the gear in his car to climb a mountain, camp in the wilderness, or trek through a snowstorm at a moment's notice.

I met Ben shortly after I moved to Colorado. He and his brother, Joe, invited me to go mountain biking. I eagerly accepted the invitation and met them in the Garden of the Gods, a beautiful park in Colorado Springs, riding my Wal-Mart fifteen-speed and anticipating a nice, easy ride in the shadow of those amazing rock formations. I quickly learned that mountain biking in Colorado actually includes mountainous terrain. Somehow, I had missed the part where going for a ride didn't mean staying on the paved walkways around the park. To this day I am grateful for the way Ben and Joe patiently waited for me as we climbed hills and avoided any trails with any measure of difficulty.

At our church, Ben joined a small group I was leading. We had many engaging discussions about what it means to follow Christ completely, and we played a lot of games of Ultimate Frisbee in the park. I got to know Ben's carefree spirit, and he became familiar with my keen ability to make a Frisbee resemble a wounded bird in flight.

There was a passion brewing in Ben that I didn't know about at first. It had begun a few years before I met him, during a time when he was praying and fasting. He sensed the Lord telling him with unshakable certainty that he was to devote his life to serving the people of Tibet.

Seven years would pass before Ben finally answered the call, but they were years of faithful preparation, not delay. He went to college, completed a year of seminary, and earned a journeyman's license as a certified electrician. He started small, worked locally, and gradually did what he needed to do to become prepared.

Before he went overseas, he gave away his beloved percussion instruments, camping gear, and most of his clothes and shoes to friends and family. Along with about forty other friends, I attended a sending-off party for Ben, where the festivities culminated in a time of worship, prayer, and moving speeches about Ben's life.

In February 2005, Ben moved to Nepal and began his efforts to reach the Tibetan people. (Nepal is open to Christians, whereas Tibet is not.) In Nepal, Ben began to learn the Tibetan language and worked in the Bhouda region of Kathmandu with a Tibetan man named James, whom he had met on a past visit. James was one of only a few Tibetan Christians, and he was passionate about bringing the message of Christ to his people. With James, Ben traveled to homes and schools, teaching music, English, and theology to the Tibetan Christians.

Then Ben learned of the Manangi people, a group of Tibetans who had settled in Nepal three or four centuries ago, in a region about fifty kilometers from the Tibetan border. They were originally Tibetan Buddhist, though over time, their faith morphed to include elements of animistic worship picked up from the Bon religion in the area. There were reports of human sacrifice among the Manangis as recently as the 1970s. Their need for Christ was as apparent as it was urgent. Getting to the Manangis, however, required crossing an 18,000-foot mountain pass. Ben made the journey several times.

By early 2006, Ben had established several inroads among the Manangi people. Ben became affiliated with the Lophel Ling school, becoming a science teacher—

and role model—to the eager Manangi children, and he befriended the old widow who ran the inn where he stayed when he was in Manang. He helped her plow her field and keep the place clean and ready for visitors.

THE COST OF SERVICE

But this life of passion and service in Nepal did not come without cost. There were times when the razor's edge of loneliness cut deeply into Ben's soul. Shortly after arriving in Nepal, he wrote in his journal:

> It's weird traveling alone. . . . I need good friends with whom I can pray, and laugh, and cry. Jesus, I ask you for close companions.[1]

Later, he wrote of his loneliness again:

> I have learned that I cannot survive alone, despite all the vain attempts of assuring everyone at home I will be just fine. I love people. I need them to live. I cannot do this without others to be with, to fight with, to stand with, to die with.

Loneliness was not his only affliction. There were physical challenges as well. After eating what a Nepalese restaurant menu called "tuna," Ben developed a high fever that confined him to his bed. At points, the fever chills were so severe that in the midst of a 65-degree day, he put on thermal underwear, a down vest, and a wooly hat and wrapped himself in his 20-degree sleeping bag. Ben, though tender in heart, endured physical hardship with little evidence of his pain. This is a guy who wrote in his journal shortly after arriving in Nepal that he was having a "difficult time spending money for things like a bed," something he thought to be "excessive." But this sickness brought so much pain that tears streamed down his face. Fighting the weakness in his body, he barely kept himself from passing out. In the midst of battling this sickness alone, he wrote:

> Told myself in a pathetic refrain, "Don't cry; be a good soldier for Jesus; don't cry. 'If you falter in the day of adversity, how small is your strength.'"[2]

A few days later, when the fever began to subside, a wave of discouragement rose to take its place. Ben wrote:

> Today I was greatly discouraged. . . . I was thinking of all the ways I could leave sooner. . . .
>
> [After a worship song came on his CD player]: Then my spirit rose and the Lord urged me to get up and worship. And then, just as fast as the fever broke, the Lord broke the discouragement that was crushing me.
>
> One thing's for sure—I've discovered that if I have anything but pure motive in following the call of the Lord here, I will not make it. So it is that I must put my hand to the plow and not turn back, listen to Your call, go where You send me.
>
> Lord, how dependent upon Your word my heart is. I will dry up and die without it.

It was listening to God's call that had led Ben to the heart of darkness in central Asia; it was his love for

God's Word and his desire to share it with others that drove him every day. It was love that made him willing to risk everything.

Ben had made his peace with risk a long time ago. While pondering the idea that "the world waits for those who take a risk," Ben wrote in his journal:

> [The world] belongs to them. They are the central figures of time—as though history is just the telling of them from one to the next.
>
> Economics—the story of those who risked money to create more;
>
> . . . Religion—the story of those who risk believing in something that could possibly be wrong;
>
> . . . Music, arts, poetry, movies, social life belong to the heart that is willing to risk;
>
> Evangelism—is the risk of rejection;
>
> Pastor—risk of leading;
>
> Inventions—all must begin with the risk of there being impossibilities;
>
> Business, millionaires, farmers, and entrepreneurs—a risk of weather, soil, seed.
>
> In all things, there are unknown factors, but the world belongs to those who embrace the unknown and risk failure to pursue greatness.

These are the words of a man who embraced risk. But the adversity he faced only refined his motivation and drew out God's voice with even more clarity. That's why when Ben's friend Ram, a Nepali believer, invited him to visit his village where there were no other Christians, Ben could not resist. Ram had come from an alcoholic family and had somehow found Christ. In an e-mail to his brother, Ben wrote:

> Brandon and I are taking [a] ride with our friend Ram
> to his village in south Nepal. It's gonna be hot. But
> a great opportunity. He is the only believer in his
> village.

Ben, his friend Brandon, and Ram traveled the two-lane road three hours south of Kathmandu. To call the two-lane roads in Nepal "highways" would be a gross over-statement. To get anywhere, one must navigate through a web of cars, bicycles, cows, people, trash, potholes, buses, trucks, and trishaws. For Ben, a motorcycle was the most sensible choice. It was the best way to get to the people he was giving his life to serve.

After three days of sharing Christ with many in Ram's village, Ben and Brandon made the drive back to Kathmandu. About an hour and a half from the city, Ben pulled into the opposite lane to get around a stalled bus. What he didn't see until it was too late was a truck trundling along in the other lane. The truck driver and Ben both swerved, but Ben's motorcycle clipped the side of the truck, flinging his body to the side of the road. By the time Brandon and Ram could reach him, Ben was already in heaven.

IN DEATH, FULLY ALIVE

What happened to Ben Couch on the morning of May 31, 2006, was not death; he had embraced Jesus' prom-ise and died to his own priorities long ago. What hap-pened that morning on the road to Kathmandu was Ben

Couch coming fully alive for the very first time, tasting the fulfillment of the promise Jesus made when he said, "Whoever wants to save his life will lose it, but whoever loses his life for me will find it."[3]

He understood the nature of lasting change. He was determined to leave an impact that outlasted his own life.

Ben understood the nature of lasting change. He was determined to be in scenes that made the Director's final cut, to leave an impact that outlasted his own life. He embraced the nature of change and acted accordingly.

It started with a dream and a passion. Ben loved Tibet and the people deeply. He loved it in the way that Christ loved the church and gave up his life to make her holy. Ben gave his heart to Ram, James, and other people he met there. He didn't love an idea or a people group. He loved individuals in real relationships, not as idealistic virtues. Because of his love, that unreasonable love, he traversed 18,000-foot mountain passes, sold his clothes, and passed through the dark valley of loneliness. Like the butterfly in flight, Ben was doing the necessary things to achieve his purpose of connecting with the people.

He knew the risks inherent in following Christ. To love at all is a risk; and loving leads to even more risk. Ben's love for Christ and for the Tibetan and Nepalese people led him to place his life in a situation of great risk. Eating the food of the locals, living with the barest of necessities, riding a motorcycle through the crowded streets of Nepal to get to the people he taught—these are not the comforts of modern living. They are not the safeties and securities of living in a country with a government that ensures that roads are paved, health care is available, and restaurants serve meals that meet a certain standard. They are not the efficiencies of a society connected by telecommunications technology, or the freedoms enjoyed by a democratic nation.

No, Ben Couch was not living in safety. He voluntarily placed himself within danger's grasp because he loved Christ, he loved the peoples of Central Asia, and he "loved not his life, even unto death." He was following Christ into one of the darkest regions of the world, and he was willing to face whatever the cost would be. He was willing to die for Christ. The proof was not in a theoretical martyrdom in which he made "the right choice"; the proof was in the way that he willingly embraced risk. He refused to live as he pleased and thereby deny Christ. Instead, he followed Christ, and embraced death.

PASSIONATE ACTION

Like Nehemiah's, Ben's passion translated into real actions. He was faithful in the small things. He acted within his reach by using the skills he had in the ways he could—teaching English and other classes. He trained as an electrician so that he would have a practical skill to apply in a place like Nepal. He took seminary classes to better prepare for the spiritual realities of the lives he would encounter. He sold almost everything that was of any value—it was all less valuable than his life, which he'd already given up—following not simply the principles of Jesus' ministry but his very words: "Sell everything you have and give to the poor, and you will have treasure in heaven."[4] But Ben didn't simply give his money to the people; he gave his life by living among them. Like a man who leaves his father and mother to be one with his wife, he took Jesus' words to heart: "If anyone comes to me and does not hate his father and mother, his wife and children, his brothers and sisters—yes, even his own life—he cannot be my disciple."[5]

Ben left the comforts of family and friends, experiencing the deep vacancy of their absence, to follow Jesus' call to Nepal. He was so in love with Jesus that he would walk with him, work with him, and go to war with him, no matter the price. He understood that Jesus was not simply a spiritual sage to be admired, or a historical figure to be studied. Jesus was a friend to be followed at all costs—at real costs. Even if they seemed like small and unnecessary sacrifices at the time, they authenticated the reality of Ben's commitment.

For Ben, Kathmandu was his Jerusalem. But, even before he could be there "working on the wall," Ben was faithfully bearing his cup in Colorado. He was not standing around, waiting for greatness or significance to fulfill his dreams. He was acting in his local context and with his heart set toward Jerusalem. Even during the years spent in Colorado, Ben was getting closer and closer to fulfilling his dream. Like Nehemiah, his passion grew for an unseen country. He faithfully nurtured his godly passion and drew from its strength as he awaited the moment when he would arrive and undertake his ultimate mission.

Ben's passion was not for some oblique ideal without a specific target. Although his work culminated thousands of miles from Colorado, it was a specific place, not a vague "out there." Instead it was "right there." He didn't spread his passion out to see where it might stick. He focused it on one place out of many—a place he identified by prayer and fasting and seeking God's direction. He invested all of his energy in one place, in one stock, taking a chance, making a commitment. And he was doing all he could to create lasting change in that one place.

Ben's focus was the result of his realization that change is local and gradual. He stayed focused. His passion didn't waver. The people of Tibet were always his focus. And he intended to stay in Nepal until his work with the Tibetan people there was done. He had no idea it would be so brief. But it did not matter, because he was less concerned about the world's notions of success and more concerned about being faithful to answer the call of God on his life. He wasn't worried about what he might or might not accomplish. His life

His life was already poured out as an offering to God, beyond re-gathering, so that it had already become a sweet aroma to God.

was already poured out as an offering to God, beyond re-gathering, so that it had already become a sweet aroma to God.[6] His actions were simply an expression of a heart and a life already fulfilling God's call.

Was Ben's life successful by society's standards? No. Was he faithful and obedient? Without a doubt. For followers of Jesus, success is simply faithfulness and obedience. God will accomplish the rest. Ben was faithful and obedient in the scenes God gave him to be in.

BEN'S LEGACY

At Ben's memorial service, Caleb—one of Ben's closest friends—stood up and called others to join with him, his wife, and their newborn son as they moved to Nepal. Specific jobs needed to be filled, posts at the school vacated by Ben's death. The words of Pastor Jabu, whom Ben had worked alongside, rang clear like a mission bell: "Ben came, he became one of us; he wore our clothes, he ate our food. He lived as we did. We need more Bens." A large group of young people responded to Caleb's call. Eventually, the number was whittled down to five young men and women who committed to go to Nepal, to hike the 18,000-foot pass, and work to reach the Manangi people.

Ben's story is a fulfillment of the words from a heavenly voice to the apostle John on the island of Patmos:

> "Write this: Blessed are those who die in the Master from now on; how blessed to die that way!"
> "Yes," says the Spirit, "and blessed rest from their hard, hard work. None of what they've done is wasted; God blesses them for it all in the end."[7]

None of what they've done is wasted. Their deeds will follow them. Their legacy will be forever. Ben Couch was like a butterfly on the other side of the world. There are many who are now a part of the tornado he started. His life and story are a call to action—not to be "successful," but to be found faithful and obedient.

WHEN GOD REMEMBERS YOU

Nehemiah and his company eventually finished the wall around Jerusalem. People began to return to their once ruined city. Through Ezra, they recovered the law and began to read it and worship again. Joy filled their homes, and strength surged in their hearts. They were becoming a nation again.

During his life, Nehemiah prayed repeatedly to be remembered by God. He had no idea how unforgettable his life would become.

During his life, Nehemiah prayed repeatedly to be remembered by God. He had no idea how unforgettable his life would become. A little less than five hundred years after Nehemiah rode his donkey into Jerusalem and scanned the rubble of burned stone and ashes, another man rode into Jerusalem, also on a donkey. When he looked around, he saw giant walls and majestic gates that towered above the crowds of people who were waving palm branches in his honor. The scene was epic; the moment was fit for a king. I wonder if in that moment, the cries of "Hosanna" were hushed in heaven's ears as Jesus whispered, "Nehemiah, I remember you. Well done, good and faithful servant."

If not for Nehemiah, there would have been no walls of Jerusalem. Without the walls of Jerusalem, the people could not have returned home. No people, no city; no city, no triumphal entry of the Messiah. Think of it: Nehemiah the wall builder was part of the story of Christ the Savior. Somehow, laying bricks and swinging hammers prepared the way for God to come to earth and redeem humanity.

Here's what we can be sure of: The kingdom of God will be established. The wall God is building will be completed. Christ will do his work and it will endure forever. The only question that remains is whether we will be involved. The choice is ours. Our legacy will be as long as our obedience.

Be faithful with the small things. Act where you are. Stay over the long haul. Multiply your efforts. Love people passionately and personally. Lay down your life in obedience to Christ. These are the marks a life remembered by God, a life that will make a world of difference.

notes

Chapter 2: Storing up Greatness

1. genesis 28:16, NLT
2. nehemiah 1:3, author's paraphrase
3. nehemiah 1:8-9, NLT

Chapter 3: History in the Making

1. henri poincaré, quoted in "chaos theory," an article on the polytechnic institute web site, home.earthlink.net/~srrobin/chaos.html.
2. 2 peter 1:4, NASB

Chapter 4: Shooting the Moon

1. mark 13:33-37, ESV

Chapter 5: All the Small Things

1. see acts 20:32, 26:18; ephesians 4:1-3; philippians 1:27; colossians 1:9-12.
2. nehemiah 2:1-2. nehemiah 2:3-4, NLT
4. nehemiah 2:5-6, NLT
5. john w. gardner, quoted by former secretary of health and human services donna shalala at the fda innovations in

government award ceremony in washington, d.c., march 3, 1998. www.hhs.gov/news/speeches/FDAinnov.html.

6. luke 16:10, NLT
7. www.quotationsbook.com/quotes/6620/view

Chapter 6: Big Dreams

1. 2 corinthians 4:8-9, NLT
2. mark 5:15, THE MESSAGE
3. mark 5:19, THE MESSAGE

Chapter 7: YourSpace

1. *the catholic encyclopedia,* www.newadvent.org/cathen/09438b.htm, paragraph 26.
2. ibid.

Chapter 8: Farewell to Fireworks

1. oswald chambers, *my utmost for his highest* (new york: dodd mead, 1935), july 6.
2. 2 peter 3:9, NIV
3. see nehemiah 2:1-8.
4. nehemiah 2:17, NLT
5. nehemiah 2:18, NLT
6. ephesians 2:10, author's adaptation from NIV text.

Chapter 9: Staying the Course

1. http://news.nationalgeographic.com/news/2003/04/0409_030409_sars.html
2. details for this story were drawn from two sources: http://news.nationalgeographic.com/news/2003/04/0409_030409_sars.html, and http://en.wikipedia.org/wiki/SARS.
3. details and quotes for this story were drawn from www.chinadaily.com.cn/en/doc/2003-05/31/content_167290.htm.

Chapter 10: Mono-Purpose Halls

1. matthew 10:39, NIV
2. luke 9:51, NLT
3. harold myra and marshall shelley, *the leadership secrets of billy graham* (grand rapids: zondervan, 2005), 68.
4. ibid., 67.
5. nehemiah 4:2, NLT
6. nehemiah 4:11, NLT

7. nehemiah 4:14, NLT
8. nehemiah 6:3, NLT
9. nehemiah 6:9, NLT

Chapter 11: Multiplied Efforts

1. james surowiecki, *the wisdom of crowds* (new york: doubleday, 2004), 70-71.
2. ibid., 71.
3. ibid.
4. ibid.
5. james white, *a brief history of christian worship* (nashville: abingdon, 1993), 41.
6. Ibid., 40.
7. luke 17:33, NLT
8. see psalm 139.
9. see colossians 1:17.
10. 1 peter 2:4-5, NLT
11. see 1 corinthians 6:19.
12. 1 corinthians 3:16, NLT
13. 1 corinthians 12:12-14, NLT
14. 1 john 4:7-8, NLT
15. 1 john 4:12, NLT
16. 1 john 4:20-21, NLT
17. ephesians 2:10, NIV

Chapter 12: Love and War

1. 1 corinthians 13:13, NLT
2. leo tolstoy, *anna karenina,* trans. richard pevear and larissa volokhonsky (new york: penguin, 2002), 375.
3. ibid., 402-403
4. ibid., 797
5. 1 john 4:18, NIV
6. ephesians 3:17-19, NIV
7. 2 peter 1:4, NASB
8. paul johnson, *intellectuals* (new york: harper & row, 1988), 28-29.
9. ibid., 29.
10. ibid., 48.
11. ibid., 31.
12. ibid., 79-80
13. nehemiah 4:11, NLT
14. nehemiah 4:12, NLT

15. nehemiah 4:14, NLT
16. nehemiah 4:19-20, NLT

Chapter 13: The Cost of Change

1. revelation 12:11, NLT
2. justo gonzáles, *the story of christianity* (san francisco: harper & row, 1984), 98-99.
3. ibid., 99.
4. ibid., 44.
5. ibid.
6. mark galli, "is persecution good for the church?" *christianity today,* may 19, 1997, www.ctlibrary.com/1195
7. gonzáles, 44.
8. galli, np.
9. psalm 116:15, NIV
10. rodney stark, *the rise of christianity* (san francisco: harper, 1997), 179.
11. john 6:54, NLT
12. john 6:67-68, NLT
13. philippians 3:8, NIV; romans 8:18, NLT; 2 corinthians 4:17, NLT

Chapter 14: Testing Your Wings

1. excerpts from ben couch's journal in this chapter are used by permission of his family.
2. proverbs 24:10, ben couch's paraphrase.
3. matthew 16:25, NIV
4. mark 10:21, NIV
5. luke 14:26, NIV
6. see philippians 2:17; 2 corinthians 2:14-15.
7. revelation 14:13, THE MESSAGE

about the author

Glenn Packiam is an associate worship pastor at New Life Church in Colorado Springs, and director of the New Life School of Worship. He is also the worship leader for New Life's college ministry, theMILL, where more than 1,200 students gather every Friday night. What this all means is that Glenn attends a lot of meetings, plays a lot of music, and drinks a lot of coffee.

Glenn is also one of the worship leaders and songwriters for Desperation Band, the worship team for New Life Church's student ministries. Desperation Band has released four albums through Integrity Music: *My Savior Lives, Who You Are, From the Rooftops,* and

Desperation. Several of Glenn's worship songs, including "Your Name," "Everyone (Praises)," "My Savior Lives," and "We Lift You Up," are fast-rising favorites in churches around the world.

Glenn and his wife, Holly, and their two adorable daughters, Sophia and Norah, enjoy life in the shadow of the Rocky Mountains.

"Your people settled in it, and from your bounty, O God, you provided for the poor." - Psalm 68:10

BE THE CHANGE

HOW LITTLE THINGS CAN MAKE A BIG DIFFERENCE — **WORLD RELIEF**

Every one of these gifts is part of a long-term project to create real and lasting change in the lives of some of the world's poorest people. These catalog items demonstrate how your gift can be used, and they illustrate the goods and services of World Relief's ministries. All gifts are designated to the country and core program described.

Choose gifts from this **Catalog of Hope** and support ministries that relieve human suffering, poverty and hunger worldwide in the name of Jesus Christ. Working with, for and from the church, World Relief's ministries enable local churches to become active in meeting the material and spiritual needs of the lost and hurting in their communities.

✓ Mail the enclosed order form to World Relief;

✓ Call toll-free 1 800 535 LIFE (5433); or

✓ Donate securely online at www.worldrelief.org.

Africa **BURKINA FASO**

Burkina Faso is one of the poorest countries in the world. Unlike many other poor African nations, it is a peaceful country with almost no history of violent conflict. There is also a high prevalence of AIDS in Burkina Faso that is compounded by poor healthcare, low literacy levels, and meager earnings.

BLESSED UNION $10.00
Allow a youth group member to participate in a retreat designed to unite and encourage members in their individual commitments to premarital abstinence.

LOOK AFTER ORPHANS $150.00
Support local church members as they care for orphans and other vulnerable children in their communities.

OFFER GUIDANCE Church $150.00
Provide guides for Sunday Schools as they lead students through biblical messages and learn more about AIDS prevention.

APPLAUD THE GOOD NEWS $200.00
Enable a dynamic Christian theatre group to travel to remote villages, educating communities about AIDS while offering God's perfect solution.

MINISTRY ON THE MOVE $1,000.00
Invest in a small motorbike or moped for church volunteers to visit terminally ill AIDS patients in their homes. The church will provide the gas!

Africa **BURUNDI**

Burundi's challenges include a political crisis that pre-dates the 1993 assassination of the country's first democratically elected president. The ongoing conflict, referred to by some as a slow-onset genocide, has resulted in massive increases in poverty and suffering.

GOOD EGGS $10.00
Buy five chickens that will lay eggs to be eaten or sold to purchase food for a malnourished child.

BREAD MAKER $42.00
Help build a clay oven for a bread baking business.

BUYING TIME $100.00
Place a cell phone in to the hands of a small business entrepreneur who can sell time to community members unable to afford their own phones.

Africa **DEMOCRATIC REPUBLIC OF CONGO**

For Congo, this poverty, coupled with decades of tyrannical leadership in the midst of ongoing regional violence, has only fueled Africa's worst war in the past 20 years.

DAILY BREAD $10.00
Help generate much-needed income by providing a family with flour, oil, sugar and charcoal to make bread to be sold.

SHELTER FROM THE STORM $15.00
Protect a widow and her children from the rain by covering a small house with straw.

BEANS $40.00
Purchase one sack of beans that can be sold by-the-bowl to help a struggling family earn extra income.

Africa **MALAWI**

Over 65 percent of Malawi's population lives below the poverty line. Increased malnutrition weakens the resistance of people infected with HIV and further reduces the workforce supporting agriculture and other trades. The number of AIDS-orphans is increasing; many of them are now cared for by relatives who are already under economic hardship.

EQUIP CHURCH LEADERS $20.00
Support Bible-based teaching that promotes abstinence among youth and fidelity in marriage while providing guidance and counseling in a country where one-in-six people live with AIDS.

A HEALTHY START $25.00
Equip churches and communities to provide vital healthcare for young children so they grow up healthy and strong.

COMMUNITY GARDENS $30.00
Help a local church plant a community vegetable garden to feed hungry families.

FIGHT FAMINE AT ITS ROOTS $42.00
Provide seeds and fertilizer to strengthen the outcome for a farmer's entire family.

Africa **MOZAMBIQUE**

Mozambique continues to recover from war and natural disaster. An internal war raged for 16 years and left people internally displaced or fleeing as refugees. In 2000, southern Mozambique experienced rising floodwaters that swept away roads, villages, schools, farmland, and the entire provincial town of Xai Xai.

READ AND WRITE $20.00
Support the purchase and translation of literacy materials to teach mothers vital life skills.

A WELLSPRING OF LIFE $25.00
Equip five Mozambican volunteers with a simple rehydration solution that can help reduce the effects of cholera and malaria.

NEW BEGINNINGS $200.00
Help six people start a small chicken-rearing project for food and economic empowerment.

BREAK GROUND $1,000.00
Help build a community center for vocational training in fields like brick-laying and carpentry.

Africa **RWANDA**

Rwanda is known as "The Land of a Thousand Hills." Despite the beauty of its people and land, Rwanda faces many struggles. It continues to recover from the tragic human and economic destruction suffered during the war and genocide in the early 1990s.

SEEDS OF HOPE $10.00
Provide seeds to people living with AIDS so they can grow nutritious food.

RADIO SPOT $30.00
Support nationwide broadcasts of AIDS prevention messages that focus on youth abstinence, fidelity in marriage, Christ-like personal behavior, and community care.

CAPITAL VENTURE $35.00
Enable a poor mother to set-up a market stall and stock it with 20 kg (44 lbs) of salt for resale in smaller quantities.

LIFE SKILLS $120.00
Provide six months of vocational training to a vulnerable orphan.

Africa **SOUTHERN SUDAN**

Sudan is geographically and culturally diverse. However, 20 years of war have destroyed much of the civil infrastructure and disrupted traditional trade, transportation, education and production systems. The war has left the population of the south highly vulnerable to famine in years with abnormal rainfall, and susceptible to common, preventable illnesses.

BUILD CAPACITY $50.00
Enable a local health worker to attend training to build their capacity to serve the community.

MOBILE HEALTH $50.00
Help protect vulnerable children through the critical age of five from major childhood diseases. Purchase a bicycle, enabling a vaccinator to reach less-accessible rural villages and (spare parts included).

SCHOOL MATERIALS $100.00
New schoolbooks specifically for the southern Sudanese have recently been published! Purchase materials to help long-neglected children.

THIRST QUENCHER $500.00
Help cover the cost of drilling a borehole to provide clean drinking water in areas where it is most needed.

Asia **CAMBODIA**

One of the poorest countries in Southeast Asia, Cambodia, has faced decades of war, with its related physical, emotional and spiritual oppression. Families are still struggling with basic needs such as adequate nutrition, shelter, immunizations for their children, and control of diarrheal diseases and pneumonia. In addition, infectious diseases such as dengue fever, malaria, and now AIDS continue to take a toll on the people.

ALIVE AT FIVE $15.00
Provide training for a health volunteer to help mothers receive vital knowledge about disease prevention and nutrition so they may nurture their children through the most vulnerable years of their lives.

SEEDS OF CHANGE $50.00
Provide a loan to help a farmer purchase and plant rice seed.

TRAIN ONE TO REACH MANY $50.00
Enable a pastor or lay leader to attend a group AIDS-training workshop and equip them to mobilize their own congregation for a compassionate response to people living with AIDS.

Asia **CHINA**

World Relief is helping to empower the Chinese Churches and NGO's to confront the AIDS threat and to prevent it from becoming a catastrophe. Community groups can uniquely minister to people, both in prevention and care, when provided with the proper resources.

HOME CARE $15.00
Distribute five *Hope at Home* manuals to guide families in supportive care for members living with AIDS.

LIGHT THE LIGHT $30.00
Cover the cost of a three-day training session for a church leader or health worker on compassionate response to the AIDS crisis.

The Americas **HAITI**

Haiti remains the poorest country in the Western Hemisphere. Its already bad economic situation has deteriorated significantly over the past several years. Conditions are rife for the spread of AIDS and women and girls are the most vulnerable.

HOT MEALS $10.00
Giving children have a hot meal every day for a month.

RESCUE CHILDREN $12.00
Provide a complete set of vaccinations for an at-risk child in the slums.

HEALTHIER FAMILIES $16.00
Help local churches share health and hygiene knowledge with mothers to improve the lives of entire families.

LIFESAVING OFFERING $27.00
Provide AIDS education, biblical counseling and care to Haitian children living with or affected by the disease.

REACHING THE SLUMS $50.00
Offer the capital for a small, wage-earning business so one family can work its way out of extreme poverty and towards a better life.

CHURCH MOBILIZATION $50.00
Provide training for one pastor or church leader to build capacity within the Church.

UNITED STATES

The United States is a nation of immigrants. America continues to welcome people fleeing persecution. Newly-arrived refugees are welcomed and provided with the essentials to meet their immediate needs. World Relief encourages them in becoming self sufficient and offers numerous classes to help them integrate with a new culture.

BREAD OF LIFE $16.00
Support the translation and distribution of a Bible in the native language of a newly-arrived refugee.

LANGUAGE SKILLS $20.00
Offer the opportunity for a refugee to learn basic English with the provision of materials and lessons – skills that are the foundation for a smooth transition to life in the United States.

AN OPEN DOOR $25.00
Support the employment authorization process for a newly-arrived immigrant.

MAKE A CONNECTION $30.00
Give a phone card so that a refugee can connect to friends and family by phone.

BACK TO SCHOOL $30.00
Provide a book bag with school supplies for a child starting school in a new place.

WARM WELCOME $30.00
Supply a refugee with a warm blanket for cold winter nights.

COVER UP $40.00
Supply a new refugee mother with a diaper bag, changing necessities and a one-week supply of diapers for her newborn to help ease them into their new environment.

PRECIOUS CARGO $800.00
Cover the cost of ten infant car seats for the legal transportation of newly-arrived refugee children.

YOU CAN CHANGE LIVES...

Pray for God's direction in all of our ministry programs

Continue to grow in the **knowledge** of the needs of the poor worldwide

Advocate for humanitarian work and refugee resettlement

Volunteer with our programs

Please consider these practical, Biblical ways to fulfill Christ's instructions to love and serve those in need. Please circle the programs you would like contribute to.

BURKINA FASO
1. Blessed Union	$10.00
2. Look After Orphans	$150.00
3. Offer Guidance (church)	$150.00
4. Applaud the Good News	$200.00
5. Ministry on the Move	$1,000.00

BURUNDI
6. Good Eggs	$10.00
7. Bread Maker	$42.00
8. Buying Time	$100.00

DEMOCRATIC REPUBLIC OF CONGO
9. Daily Bread	$10.00
10. Shelter from the Storm	$15.00
11. Beans	$40.00

MALAWI
12. Equip Church Leaders	$20.00
13. A Healthy Start	$25.00
14. Community Gardens	$30.00
15. FIght Famine at Its Roots	$42.00

MOZAMBIQUE
16. Reach & Teach	$10.00
17. Read & Write	$20.00
18. A Wellspring of life	$25.00
19. New Beginnings	$200.00
20. Break Ground	$1,000.00

RWANDA
21. Seeds of Hope	$10.00
22. Radio Spot	$30.00
23. Capital Venture	$35.00
24. Life Skills	$120.00

SOUTHERN SUDAN
25. Build Capacity	$50.00
26. Mobile Health	$150.00
27. School Materials (one class)	$100.00
28. Thirst Quencher	$500.00

CAMBODIA
29. Alive at Five	$15.00
30. Train One to Reach Many	$50.00
31. Seeds of Change	$50.00

CHINA
32. Home Care	$15.00
33. Light the Light	$30.00

HAITI
34. Hot Meals	$10.00
35. Rescue Children	$12.00
36. Healthier Families	$16.00
37. Lifesaving Offering	$27.00
38. Reaching the Slums	$50.00
39. Church Mobilization	$50.00

UNITED STATES
40. Bread of Life	$16.00
41. Language Skills	$20.00
42. An Open Door	$25.00
43. Make a Connection	$30.00
44. Warm Welcome	$30.00
45. Back to School	$30.00
46. Cover Up	$40.00
47. Precious Cargo	$800.00

Grand Total $ _____

PLEASE PRINT YOUR INFORMATION: GE20

Name: _____

Address: _____

City: _____ State: _____ Zip: _____

Phone: _____ Email: _____

PAYMENT INFORMATION

Please mail this form, with your **check or money order made payable to World Relief**. Or provide your credit card information below.

☐ Discover ☐ Mastercard ☐ Visa ☐ American Express

Credit Card Number _____ Exp Date: _____

Signature: _____

Please cut here

WORLD RELIEF ✚🖐
7 E Baltimore St • Baltimore MD 21202
800 535 5433 • worldrelief.org